Presentation
READY

Presentation READY

12

Improve Your Sales Presentation Outcomes & Avoid the Twelve Most Common Mistakes

TERRI L. SJODIN

Copyright © 2024 by Terri L. Sjodin. All rights reserved. Printed in the United States of America. Except as permitted under the United States Copyright Act of 1976, no part of this publication may be reproduced or distributed in any form or by any means, or stored in a database or retrieval system, without the prior written permission of the publisher.

1 2 3 4 5 6 7 8 9   LCR   29 28 27 26 25 24

ISBN   978-1-266-02161-9
MHID   1-266-02161-2

e-ISBN 978-1-266-02562-4
e-MHID   1-266-02562-6

This publication is designed to provide accurate and authoritative information in regard to the subject matter covered. It is sold with the understanding that neither the author nor the publisher is engaged in rendering legal, accounting, securities trading, or other professional services. If legal advice or other expert assistance is required, the services of a competent professional person should be sought.

—From a Declaration of Principles Jointly Adopted by a Committee of the American Bar Association and a Committee of Publishers and Associations

McGraw Hill books are available at special quantity discounts to use as premiums and sales promotions or for use in corporate training programs. To contact a representative, please visit the Contact Us pages at www.mhprofessional.com.

McGraw Hill is committed to making our products accessible to all learners. To learn more about the available support and accommodations we offer, please contact us at accessibility@mheducation.com. We also participate in the Access Text Network (www.accesstext.org), and ATN members may submit requests through ATN.

To Jim, with love.

Thank you for being my rock (and my favorite geologist). xoxo

Contents

Preface	. . . .	ix
Introduction	. . . .	xiii

SECTION I	**Case**	
MISTAKE #1	"Winging It"	3
MISTAKE #2	Being Overly Informative Versus Persuasive. .	17
MISTAKE #3	Providing Inadequate Support	31
MISTAKE #4	Failing to Close the Sale	41

SECTION II	**Creativity**	
MISTAKE #5	Misusing the Allotted Time	53
MISTAKE #6	Being Boring, Boring, Boring.	73
MISTAKE #7	Ineffectively Using Visual Aids	85
MISTAKE #8	Failure to Create Connection with Listeners. .	99

SECTION III	**Delivery**	
MISTAKE #9	Distracting Gestures and Body Language . .	117
MISTAKE #10	Dressing Inappropriately or Unprofessionally	129
MISTAKE #11	Technology or Demonstration Failures.	139
MISTAKE #12	Verbal Missteps.	155

viii CONTENTS

CONCLUSION	Performance Tips and Conducting a Self-Evaluation	167
APPENDIX A	Research and Methodology	179
APPENDIX B	Forms	183
Acknowledgments		191
Bibliography		193
Index		197

Preface

I founded Sjodin Communications in 1990 with one goal in mind: to help people build and deliver more polished, persuasive, and effective presentations that generate consistent results.

Time is a factor when I'm working with people who feel a sense of urgency around the success of their next meeting or presentation. My clients typically request quick analysis and simple, direct solutions to help improve their outcomes.

As a result, after more than a decade of working directly with sales organizations, in 2001 I developed and shared a list of the most common sales presentation mistakes that professionals make. That list ultimately became the foundation for my book *Sales Speak: The 9 Biggest Sales Presentation Mistakes & How to Avoid Them*, as well as the spin-off book *Small Message, Big Impact*.

Since the release of *Sales Speak*, I have evaluated thousands of presentations in various formats. The skills necessary to craft a winning persuasive presentation are largely constant. Still, emerging marketplace trends make revising the original work critical to keeping those we serve up to date.

Are the original mistakes in *Sales Speak* still issues of consequence? If so, why? If not, why not? Have time and technology helped us alleviate and eliminate these issues? Are things better or worse for today's presenters and their listeners, buyers, and audiences?

The answers might surprise you.

How Did We Do It?

Adopting the no-research-about-us-without-us–type approach, my team and I designed a simple survey to be completed only by professionals whose livelihoods depend on their ability to build and deliver persuasive presentations. Their responses, which were based on self-reported data, reflect what these sales professionals are thinking, doing, and seeing in the field on a regular basis.

Our initial findings were quite interesting. We found that today's sales professionals are *still* making the original 9 presentation mistakes and that the original list of 9 has grown to 12. And there was more.

Energized and intrigued, our team committed to a deeper dive, which led to a formal research study. I shared our data with a colleague at San Diego State University, Dr. Heather Canary, who heads up the SDSU School of Communication. With her guidance and insight, Sjodin Communications conducted an 18-month research effort. (In full disclosure, SDSU is my alma mater—Go Aztecs!)

The team developed the next phase of the research with Dr. Rachael Record, a social scientist and professor also in the SDSU School of Communication. Her involvement was critical in helping us develop a more comprehensive survey, execute the process properly, and analyze the data for conclusions. The project continued to focus on working sales professionals, surveying more than 2,500 people who regularly engage in selling a product, a service, or a cause.

On March 4, 2020, we proudly released the formal research results report: *The State of Sales Presentations*. Little did we know how important that work would be in helping people navigate the use of virtual presentations during the coronavirus pandemic, which was declared shortly thereafter.

Like our clients, we had to reimagine our business and our presentations. After the pandemic started, I spent much of my time reviewing countless virtual sales calls and meetings, "lunch and learns," and product demonstrations to help our clients figure out what was working out there and what was not.

We leaned on the Phase One data, as video platforms were emerging as the dominant tool for people to present. We could see additional data that deserved exploration. It was clear that a Phase Two version of the research was necessary to examine and understand the effect of virtual platform presentations.

As the stoic philosopher Seneca said, "Luck is when preparedness meets opportunity." We used the lockdown to our advantage and captured data that has revealed insights unique to presenting during that challenging time. We learned more about how to navigate specific obstacles in virtual presentations.

When the world started to return to in-person presentation opportunities, things morphed again, indicating a need for a Phase Three study to examine and prepare for the future of presenting in all its forms: in person, virtual, or a hybrid of the two. We completed that final study and are pleased to share some of the cumulative results in this book.

San Diego State University researchers analyzed both quantitative and qualitative survey results for this study, using appropriate statistical tests to analyze quantitative results. The data analyst for the Phase Two and Phase Three projects was Giuliano McDonald, first as a graduate student in the School of Communication at San Diego State University and later as a doctoral student and lecturer in the School of Communication at the University of Miami. You can access research summary reports at www.sjodincommunications.com.

The tremendous benefit of the study findings and this book is that we can *cut to the chase* and pinpoint the most glaring problems for our readers. The findings are rooted in the *self-identified* mistakes of active business and sales professionals, as well as the observations of others. They can help *all* professionals—even seasoned veterans of the industry—to pinpoint and address specific issues. I have always believed that paying close attention to those who have gone before you can and will save you time, money, and sanity, plus give you greater security moving forward.

Our isolation of the 12 mistakes, or "pain points," is particularly effective in helping readers improve quickly. An accessible read, this book is formulated for the busy professional. It is a cumulative work based on my 30-plus years of consulting in this area. The discussion is tactical and practical, and while it's not a motivational book, I hope readers will feel inspired to improve—and there's nothing more motivating than more wins!

I confess that I have personally made every one of the mistakes listed in this book at one time or another. I have seen amazing presenters when they are really "on," and I have seen them when they are "off." We all have good days and bad days, and that's okay. I am not a perfect speechwriter, speech coach, or sales presenter. Far from it. The good news is that you really don't have to be perfect to be effective.

Here's one thing I know for sure: This material will help you quickly evaluate challenges in your presentations and make simple corrections that can expand your influence and generate better outcomes.

TS

Introduction

The Backstory

I believe passionately in the power of the spoken word. No email, text message, or viral video will replace it. One person sharing an authentic, compelling message with a receptive listener, in real time, can shift everything. That's why helping people embrace the art of persuasive speaking has been my life's work.

For me, that road started with competitive forensics. My years on speech and debate teams in high school and college were fun and impactful. This activity involves participants engaging in different kinds of public speaking events during tournaments. Debate involves creating a specific speech and a plan—with an affirmative side and a negative side to an assigned topic. Individual events are more like track and field, but for various speech activities. Students who compete in this "sport" learn incredible life skills that help develop their research, analysis, communication, and persuasive abilities. I know at my core that this experience changed my life. I am a full-blown "speech geek."

One thing I learned early on about participating in speech tournaments was that winning had little to do with where you went to school, what neighborhood you lived in, or how much experience you had. There were no matching uniforms, and when you arrived at the event, you were given a number. A handful of competitors went to a room where they stood up one at a time and gave their speech to a judge. It was fascinating and highly competitive.

xiv INTRODUCTION

If you had the highest-ranked speech in the preliminary rounds, you moved on to the next round. If not, you were done. It was that simple. The presenter with the best speech prevailed. You got immediate feedback, for better or worse.

Whenever I was eliminated, I stuck around to watch the semifinal and final rounds to pay attention to what was landing with the audience and the judges. Then I tried to figure out why my own speech was not as effective. I took a guess at what was not working, then went to the next tournament with a stronger speech and more polished delivery. I kept testing new approaches through trial and error.

The key takeaway? *You don't keep competing in the next tournament with a speech that does not win.* That same principle applies in business and sales. If a pivotal presentation doesn't move you forward, you've got to figure out why and change it.

Most people want to improve their presentations but don't know where to start. And that can be costly. As a speech geek, I have always known this to be true. I have spent the better part of my career reviewing presentations and conducting formal research to apply this work in the professional world.

Of course, everyone's personal "speech and debate tournament scenario" is different. Maybe you have the rare opportunity to connect with a sought-after CEO to promote your idea or a cause. Perhaps you are facing an interview for your dream job. Maybe you are competing for an exclusive client contract. Just as you don't keep going to the next tournament with a speech that doesn't win, you don't keep going back into the field with a sales presentation that doesn't close deals.

That is where this book will help you. It does the heavy lifting for you and eliminates the guesswork by identifying the most common presentation mistakes being made today. Why focus on mistakes? Because you can't improve what you don't recognize as a problem. While learning the pitfalls may be interesting, they are of little benefit if you don't see how to avoid and correct them in your own life. If you want to improve your outcomes, you need practical solutions. This work provides specific solutions and guides you through an easy process of crafting an improved presentation to use at your very next meeting.

Your Opportunity

We've all been there. An opportunity presents itself. You have one chance to share your message with a key decision maker, and the pressure mounts. At the same time, you are excited about the possibilities in front of you if all goes well.

Will you be ready? Or will you just wing it?

When you make the most of that important meeting, your path could change forever. In this age of information overload, no business skill is more essential than being able to present well, get to the point, and connect with others quickly.

Are you presenting in person, over the telephone, via a videoconferencing platform, or in some hybrid scenario? What will you say? How will you say it?

Now imagine that you deliver a clear, convincing, and creative presentation. The listener is intrigued, and the real conversation begins. Your message lands, and you get the next appointment, you win the job, you earn the sale, your network expands, or you gain support for your cause!

You might be quietly wondering if that's truly possible. The answer is yes. There is a way to eliminate the pressure and the guesswork. You do not have to wing it. There is a strategic framework to get you there, one that will help you avoid some of the most common mistakes when planning for your next presentation opportunity. When you use it, you will put yourself head and shoulders above your competition.

Like a doctor who studies your bloodwork before an appointment, what if you could ascertain your presentation's weak spots and prescribe a course of treatment? Wouldn't you want to know ahead of time before something became an issue of concern in a competitive sales presentation?

xvi INTRODUCTION

Whether you are in need of a few minor adjustments or major surgery, this book will help you bring your persuasive presentation skills to optimal health. Think of it as a checkup with 12 painless remedies of preventive or curative medicine.

> From the errors of others, a wise
> [person] corrects their own.
>
> —PUBLILIUS SYRUS

The State of Sales Presentations Research Study

As described in the Preface, underpinning the 12 common mistakes is a multiyear, three-phase, formal research study that explores this question: "Does making a sales presentation mistake impact the outcome or the ability to move a transaction forward?" The entirety of the data was self-reported by business and sales professionals. This unique data set is powerful because of the participants' transparency, and the study's specific targeting of people whose livelihoods depend on making persuasive presentations.

When conducting the research, we also collected information about the habits, perspectives, and outcomes of rookies and veterans in the sales presentation space. You will read about the participants' field experiences, both as presenters and as listeners, and learn how to navigate presentation opportunities from a different perspective. It is said that truth is stranger than fiction, and some of the stories might make you laugh or cringe, so the names of people and organizations have been removed to respect those who were willing to share their personal ailments. The goal of this book is not to discourage or alarm but to enlighten and equip presenters. As you read this book for the first time, you may find some issues that are not your issues. You might think, "that's me," or "that's not me." That's okay. Start by working on mistakes that are most relevant to you and focus on improving in those areas.

Does Making a Sales Presentation Mistake Matter?

One of the most surprising initial insights in the research was that 92 percent of participants reported feeling that making a presentation mistake has or probably has impacted moving a transaction forward or achieving their goal. Does making a sales presentation mistake matter? Our research says yes.

A significant portion of a business development professional's day is spent communicating verbally; yet about 55 percent of the participants reported receiving little to no presentation skills training over the course of their careers. This gap in training may contribute to the study's findings.

Key Research Findings

The study notes 12 mistakes that participants consistently self-identified and observed in others.

This graph presents a comparative analysis of how sales professionals perceive their own mistakes in addition to those they recognized in their peers.

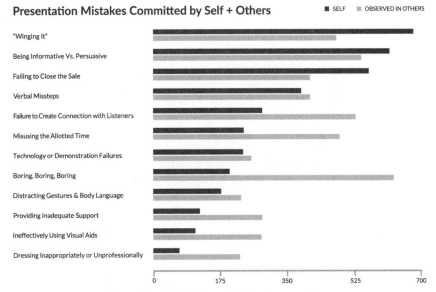

Phase Three of the State of Sales Presentations:
A total of 1,075 individuals completed the survey.

xviii INTRODUCTION

The top three self-reported presentation mistakes, ranked by frequency, were as follows:

- ▶ "Winging it"
- ▶ Being informative versus persuasive
- ▶ Failing to close the sale

Note: The top three self-reported mistakes were the same in all three phases of the research study.

Key findings also included these:

- ▶ The number one presentation mistake that participants reported seeing *others* make was being boring, boring, boring.
- ▶ 88 percent of study participants reported that seeing someone make a presentation mistake made them *less likely to work with that person.*
- ▶ 86 percent reported that seeing someone make a presentation mistake made them *less likely to buy from or move forward with that person's company.*
- ▶ 92 percent reported that their own presentation mistakes probably held them back from achieving their goals.
- ▶ 99.9 percent reported making at least one presentation mistake over the past six months. The median was three significant mistakes.
- ▶ In the entire study, just one person reported making no mistakes.
- ▶ In all three phases of the study, professionals continued to make all 12 mistakes whether in person, on videoconferencing platforms, or in hybrid formats—regardless of their gender, generation, or whether they were selling a product, service, or cause.

The following research observations are also of importance to presenters:

- ▶ Today's sales professionals are best served when they are proficient at all three presentation formats and able to pivot between them with ease.

- ▶ While there are limitations to virtual and hybrid presentations, these formats also have the advantages of convenience and increased access to listeners. In many ways, it can be easier to gather key decision makers in the same virtual room than to arrange a logistically complicated, in-person meeting.

- ▶ Where a professional is in the sales process—as well as listener and audience preferences—will determine presentation modality.

As you will see throughout this book, the research demonstrates that even in the face of groundbreaking technological advances and unbelievable change, selling and presenting are primarily about human interaction and connection. The key to that connection is delivering your message in the most clear, concise, and compelling manner, within an appropriate amount of time, whether presenting in person, via a videoconferencing platform, or in a hybrid format.

Moving Ahead

Some people sell a product, some a service, some a cause, but they all are looking for the secret that moves the needle, drives conversion, or makes someone say "Yes!" When sales professionals have pivotal presentations coming up, they typically want a quick tip for success: "I have a big meeting coming up. What's the one thing I need to know?"

It's not one thing. It's three things: a great presentation reflects a solid *case*, thoughtful *creativity*, and engaging *delivery*. The content of this book is divided into these three benchmarks:

Section I—Case

Case speaks to the foundation of your persuasive arguments and content. It includes evidence, analytics, logic, and the ability to craft a message that moves a listener to a desired outcome.

Section II—Creativity

Creativity addresses how your persuasive message resonates with listeners. It relies on storytelling, visual aids, structure, curiosity, and the way you customize your language to meet your audience's needs.

Section III—Delivery

Delivery includes the elements of your overall performance effort. It features your unique style, movement, personality, and ability to execute effectively.

Under each of these three benchmarks are the four most common mistakes in that area that can cost presenters an opportunity. This book blends research, peer-to-peer insights, humble confessions, and thoughtful real-world observations to help you learn vicariously from the experiences of others. Each chapter also provides concrete solutions to these real-world problems. In the Conclusion is a Speech/Presentation Evaluation Form to help you review practice presentations and set yourself up for success before your next opportunity.

These are challenging times; my goal is to help you consistently perform at your best, no matter what is happening in the market around you. When you apply this book's game-changing insights and strategies, your message will emerge clearer and more polished. Perhaps most importantly, you will be prepared for the opportunities you "never saw coming."

A presentation doesn't have to be perfect to work. It simply has to work for the circumstances you are in. There is wiggle room, and serendipity plays a role. In the end, it's about doing the best you can with the time you have. This book will help you to do that.

Let's go!

SECTION I
CASE

Case speaks to the foundation of your persuasive arguments and content. It includes evidence, analytics, logic, and the ability to craft a message that moves a listener to a desired outcome.

MISTAKE #1

"Winging It"

DEFINITION

"Winging it" is improvising, ad-libbing, or generally conducting a presentation without much preparation. First used in 1885, this term originates from the theater and refers to actors studying their parts in the wings in case they are suddenly called on to replace another performer.

Understanding Why "Winging It" Is a Mistake

According to the State of Sales Presentations research study discussed in the Introduction, "winging it" was among the top three mistakes people reported making during their sales presentations. Study participants also reported feeling that making this mistake had, or probably had, kept them from moving a transaction forward or achieving their goal.

Why does "winging it" happen so often? It's an easy play for busy professionals. It happens when you've procrastinated or simply haven't prepared ahead of time. Maybe it stems from overconfidence or misguided excitement. Whatever its origins, "winging it" rarely yields optimal results.

To some degree, the sales process will always be flexible and a little uncertain. Persuasive presentations, however, seldom materialize out of thin air. They require hard work and analysis, and must be researched, shaped, tested, and retested over time. It can be tempting to just step out in front of an audience, start speaking, and hope for the best. You might even get away with it if you are a talented, experienced speaker. If not, you can easily lose your audience.

Sometimes a seasoned pro gets thrown a curveball and manages to field it skillfully in the moment, without a hitch. There are also times when a seasoned pro relies too heavily on past experience and isn't prepared for a new situation in a different industry or with a different type of client. There's a critical difference between being able to pivot and respond extemporaneously in the moment when necessary and simply reacting without carefully considering the issue at hand. Look at the scores of sales professionals who were great at in-person sales but had to adapt to virtual presentations via video platforms almost overnight at the onset of the coronavirus pandemic. It was immediately evident that in person and virtual presentations are not the same and require different skill sets. The professionals who successfully navigated the changed landscape recognized the differences between virtual, in person, and hybrid interactions and took the time to learn how to effectively connect with listeners through a camera lens. Today this ability has gone from commonplace to expected.

A Few Real-World Confessions

We asked study participants to share their experiences and observations as both listeners and presenters. They revealed not only what they said and did in their own presentations, but also what they heard while attending other people's talks, thus providing valuable dual insights about what constitutes a successful persuasive presentation. The results showed that sales professionals who committed the mistake of "winging it" consistently failed to (1) prepare, (2) practice, and (3) get into the right frame of mind. Simply put, they did not do their homework. As a result, they appeared disorganized, unskilled, and distracted.

Let's take a closer look at some real-world examples and explore the best ways to avoid these issues.

SCENARIO 1

Presenter's Confession. *I procrastinated and waited until the last minute to get ready. I did not work through the best flow and key talking points before the meeting. I should have thought through my strategy.*

Listener's Observation. *The presenter seemed like they threw this thing together at the last minute. It felt unorganized and off point. They seemed unprepared and like they were out of their league.*

Solution. Prepare Before the Presentation

The best game plan is to do your homework early in the process, while keeping the end goal in mind. Preparation is the best way to avoid "winging it." That might seem obvious. The truth is that many people, for various reasons, simply fail to do it or don't have a strategy to prepare effectively.

Consider a meeting you have on your calendar right now and ask yourself a few key questions. *What is my intention for this meeting? What am I trying to accomplish? Who are the listeners? What's the audience size?* Use the Presentation Opportunity General Information Form that follows on the next page.

6 PRESENTATION READY

Presentation Ready

PRESENTATION OPPORTUNITY GENERAL INFORMATION FORM

I. WHAT IS THE GOAL (OR INTENTION) OF YOUR PRESENTATION?

....

....

II. AUDIENCE ANALYSIS INFORMATION

- Who are the listeners? ....
- Audience size? ....
- Average age of group? ....
- Gender ratio? ....
- Attitude of audience? ....
- How informed is the audience? ....

III. LOGISTICAL INFORMATION

- In person, virtual, or hybrid ....
- Visual aid options ....
- Time allotted for presentation ....
- Who speaks before/after you ....

IV. WHAT IS THE BEST WAY TO CLOSE IN THIS SITUATION?

....

....

Once you have answered these questions, determine your presentation's structure and format, which are vital to managing both time and content and will be discussed later. On the issue of time—there is a connection between the amount of time you will be given to present and the amount of time you will need to prepare. As Winston Churchill noted:

> If you want me to speak for two minutes, it will take me three weeks of preparation. If you want me to speak for thirty minutes, it will take me a week to prepare. If you want me to speak for an hour, I'm ready right now.
>
> —WINSTON CHURCHILL

Formats

Selecting an appropriate format is the first step to avoiding the tendency to wing it. With a specific format in mind, it's easier to prepare and proceed. If you want to give a good presentation, you must spend time preparing for it.

There are four types of speaking formats:

1. **Impromptu.** Speaking without physical prompts, but using a simple mental outline to speak in the moment.
2. **Extemporaneous.** Speaking with the aid of a written outline.
3. **Manuscript.** A presentation delivered word for word from a written document.
4. **Memorized.** The presentation is rehearsed and recited from memory.

Let's take a detailed look at each format.

Impromptu

Impromptu means that you are speaking from a mental outline and have already formulated what you want to include. Giving an impromptu talk

8 PRESENTATION READY

allows you more freedom to interact with the audience. Do it well, and this style can show how knowledgeable you are about your subject in a more conversational manner.

On the other hand, an impromptu talk has distinct disadvantages when you are trying to persuade your audience. Recalling and selecting just the right words to describe what you are talking about can be a challenge. Someone giving an impromptu talk might be mistaken by the audience for someone who is "winging it," but the two are quite different in that the former requires preparation. When you are "winging it," you are just rolling in hot and doing the best you can in the moment. When speaking impromptu, you have a mental outline that allows you the freedom to pivot as necessary.

Extemporaneous

An *extemporaneous* presentation is one you prepare in advance and deliver from an outline. To clarify, this type of presentation is not written out word for word. This is the most common format for business professionals because it allows the presenter to adjust the presentation when questions arise.

Extemporaneous means you are speaking from a physical document, usually just a single page or two—and you can easily provide a copy to the listeners you are addressing. This format is ideal when you are speaking to prospects. When you have the outline in front of you, it's unlikely you will walk out the door saying to yourself, "Oh no, I forgot to cover something!" The outline also helps keep your audience on track, following what you are saying.

Many business meetings and collateral materials have become digital, and people are directed to websites, videos, and other virtual forms of media more often than ever before. That means a physical, single-page handout can become a significant presentation piece. Why? Because your listeners can own it. They own it because they can put their personal notes on it, and they are more likely to hold on to a thing for which they feel ownership. A handout keeps your listeners involved. Better yet, it helps them to retain more information from your presentation.

The drawbacks of the extemporaneous format include the possibility of forgetting words that are necessary to nail down arguments precisely. If you have ever stumbled during a presentation while trying to find the right word, you understand the problem. The presentation can also become lopsided if the speaker spends too much time on the beginning and rushes through the second half to meet time constraints.

Manuscript

In a *manuscript* format, the entire presentation is written out word for word. Speakers then read every word of the presentation. What you say is exactly what you intended to say. You know the precise, compelling language you have prepared, and you can keep the presentation within fixed time limits. The manuscript format is often used to deliver important messages, perhaps from a government spokesperson or at a scientific seminar.

Disadvantages include the likelihood that the discourse will sound like an essay, since people rarely write the way they speak. The talk may also sound stiff. This format makes it difficult to react spontaneously to listeners and requires a great deal of preparation so that you sound natural, not canned.

Memorized

A *memorized* presentation is written in manuscript form and committed to memory. While this format was often used in the past, today most salespeople prefer the extemporaneous style. There is a benefit to using the memorized format as a starting point because it allows you to focus on your message and provide thoughtful illustrations. It is particularly effective in formal presentations. However, it requires extensive practice and commitment because if your mind goes blank—that's a problem. Enough said.

An effective exercise in a training environment is to record members of your team responding to a prospect's or listener's common objections. When people realize how often certain objections occur, they can see how much more persuasive they could be if only they practice and memorize compelling responses ahead of time.

Consider the example of Colette from Resource Dynamics. She was a new sales rep for the organization and had come from an entirely different business channel. Although she was familiar with the industry, she did not know how to overcome some of the objections she was getting over the telephone when trying to set appointments. Colette chose to shadow a seasoned colleague, listening to her manage client phone calls. Colette particularly admired the way her counterpart handled objections and wondered how she could incorporate the same specific language into her calls. Although it helped to listen to the calls in real time, she did not have ready access to the many responses needed to overcome all the varied questions and objections after just one visit.

As a solution, the two women worked together and made audio recordings of responses to prospects' questions and objections. They did this on several calls and then had the recordings transcribed. Colette later took the transcription, edited it, and posted a list of objections and responses, set in large type, on the wall by her desk for easy reference while making her calls. If a prospect had an objection, she could look right up at the appropriate response. After a while, the responses became ingrained, and she was able to take down the written responses. This simple strategy worked beautifully! Preparing your answers to questions in advance can be very useful, particularly when you don't have much time during a call and need a fast comeback.

Choosing Your Format

A good presentation requires a great deal of preparation. This is particularly true when you want to tailor your talk to each individual audience or prospect. You may have a single talk for several audiences, but it will be more effective if you take the time to customize portions of it to meet the needs of the specific group you are addressing.

As you determine your format and put together your presentation, consider:

- Are you delivering a monologue with Q&A at the end or having more of a conversation with a prospect or client? Or a little bit of both?
- Have you determined which format will help you communicate the specific points in your message?
- Is it appropriate to give a hard copy or send an email version of your outline as a handout to your listeners before your meeting?

No matter which format you choose, keep track of where you are headed with your arguments. Even the most seasoned professionals can stray off course. Be sure to prepare! When you wing it, you are more likely to spend too much time on irrelevant issues and omit or underemphasize essential points.

SCENARIO 2

Presenter's Confession. *I did not think about doing a scrimmage in advance. I was overly confident in my years of experience, and my traditional presentation did not work on a virtual platform. I wanted to be in the moment, and it backfired.*

Listener's Observation. *The speaker seemed like they were "winging it." It was hard to follow their train of thought. It was clear they were struggling with presenting virtually. It felt like their first videoconference call.*

Solution. Practice to Level Up

The market is dynamic. When there is a lot riding on the message, conducting a scrimmage in advance can be extremely helpful. We all benefit when we practice to polish our skills. Practice might be simply taking the time to think through a presentation, setting up a strategic visit with a mentor or colleague, or watching a successful presentation by a peer. Staging a full-on scrimmage in which you deliver your talk—either in person or via video platform—to trusted friends or colleagues and receive feedback about your content and flow can be invaluable. We provide specific tools to help you practice more effectively in the Conclusion.

SCENARIO 3

Presenter's Confession. *It was a big opportunity, and I was not in the right frame of mind before the meeting. I had a lot of negative chatter in my head.*

Listener's Observation. *They seemed very distracted. They wandered off topic and failed to recover.*

Solution. Focus Your Energy and Effort on the Task in Front of You

Take the time to get your head in the game. Success doesn't start when you get into the meeting—it starts well before that. There's a reason why teams get into a huddle and psych themselves up before they run out onto the court or field. Take some time to clear your mind and put other distractions aside. People who shared this confession offered illustrations that ranged from dealing with personal issues that threw them off before they even walked into a meeting, to feeling intimidated about the opportunity or by the person they were meeting with. To overcome such issues, as the saying goes, strive to "starve your distractions and feed your focus."

It only takes a minute to take a deep breath, get yourself centered, and focus your energy and effort on the task at hand. Visualize a good outcome.

In your self-talk, always clarify your intention. Circle back to the questions asked on the Presentation Opportunity General Information Form: *What is my intention for this meeting? What am I trying to accomplish? Who are the listeners? How can I be of service? What do I bring to the table that nobody else can do? What is the best way to close in this situation?* Proceed with the confidence that you have researched, shaped, tested, and retested your talk and that you are equipped with every response you will need.

> When you come from a place of hope,
> good things can come to you.
> —UNKNOWN

A Bit of Pushback
What If I Have No Time to Prepare?

What if you don't have the time necessary to put together an effective presentation? Or if an opportunity has just presented itself, and you're forced to wing it? The secret lies in carefully planning what you might want to say in a spontaneous situation. Have multiple go-to arguments, phrases, and pieces of evidence that you can count in on these situations. Memorize them, practice them in front of a mirror or on camera, and get so familiar with them that they become natural, intuitive responses.

Consider a WNBA star who's able to consistently sink critical three-pointers in a game. She can do that because she put in the time beforehand. She has done the homework, practiced relentlessly, and pushed herself through drill after drill until muscle memory takes over and she can improvise beautifully on the court.

Always keep your intention in mind, not only for a specific presentation but also when you strike up a conversation with someone you don't know. Simply keep your message out there. Believe in it, share it, and eventually it will become a natural part of your communication.

14 PRESENTATION READY

At the same time, life is unpredictable. Even when you are solidly focused on your intention, plans can go sideways. Brad McMillen, a former state championship quarterback turned internet sales executive, offered this analogy:

> As quarterback, I would go to the line, ready to throw a pass. I had a system of reads, depending on the defense. The first option was to throw long. If that was covered, as I dropped back to throw, I looked at my secondary option. If he was covered, I threw to my third option. If he was covered, I just threw the ball away or ran for my life. In the end, I kept the same overall intention: score points with my team. This progression is called checking down, and it is what quarterbacks do. They check down but always with the goal of getting to the end zone. The point is you don't have to score on every play, just advance the ball. Similarly, the point of an introductory meeting is not to just close the deal in the first appointment. Its goal is to advance you to the next point in your sales process.

This same principle applies to most professional presentation opportunities. You don't have to score on every play. Just advance the ball.

Summary

Mistake #1 is "winging it": improvising, ad-libbing, or generally conducting a presentation without much preparation.

- Research shows that "winging it" is among the top three mistakes that people reported making during their sales presentations.

- The solution is to prepare, practice, and channel your energy and effort into the task in front of you.

- You can choose from four types of speaking format options: (1) impromptu, (2) extemporaneous, (3) manuscript, and (4) memorized.

- Consider building a collection of go-to statements, phrases, and pieces of evidence that you can memorize so you will be better prepared for handling objections or out-of-the-blue opportunities.

▶ **Next Up.** Mistake #2: Being Overly Informative Versus Persuasive

MISTAKE #2

Being Overly Informative Versus Persuasive

DEFINITION

Overloading a presentation with an excessive amount of information—often without the proper context or explanation, failing to balance facts and data with an effective argument or point. This is also called data dumping.

Understanding the Issue of Being Overly Informative Versus Persuasive

This chapter discusses one of the highest ranked mistakes self-identified in our research study: being far too informative rather than persuasive. (For specific rankings, refer to the frequency table in the Introduction.) Selling can be challenging. But it is a mistake to think that the way to improve your closing ratio is to dump so much information on a listener that the person feels obligated to do business with you.

The unfortunate truth is that some listeners will use you as an information source, then use all that intel to negotiate another deal somewhere else. For example, have you ever felt that prospects seem curious about your offering, and maybe they even compliment you on your informative presentation, but they rarely seem to say yes or move forward? What we need to acknowledge is that while sales professionals might be seen as helpful when they communicate all this information, this strategy can also undermine their best efforts. Why? It doesn't efficiently drive decision-making or conversion.

Some speakers find it far easier to deliver an informative talk rather than a persuasive one. Sharing information simply feels less daunting. A manager, potential customer, friend, or neighborhood group is less likely to say no when listening to someone simply disseminating information. The problem is that they don't typically say yes either.

Professionals in need of results are best served when they craft presentations that are both persuasive and informative. Their talks create and identify needs rather than just covering the "standard needs analysis." They think proactively, not reactively, and design presentations that anticipate buyer objections so they can overcome them before objections become reasons not to buy.

A Few Real-World Confessions

We asked our study participants to share their experiences and observations as both listeners and presenters. They revealed not only what they said and did during their own presentations, but also what they witnessed in their colleagues' talks, providing valuable dual insights about what constitutes a successful persuasive presentation. The results showed that sales professionals who were too informative versus persuasive consistently failed to:

1. Get clear on the goal of being persuasive
2. Craft a message using a persuasive formula with clear arguments and distinctive talking points

As with any mistake, to avoid making it, one must understand how it manifests in the real world. Let's explore what some individuals said about being data dumpers and the victims of data dumps.

MISTAKE #2: BEING OVERLY INFORMATIVE VERSUS PERSUASIVE **19**

SCENARIO 1

Presenter's Confession. *I wanted to give them a complete overview and understanding of what we can do. I confess I may have lingered too long in the information zone. Sometimes I feel like if I just provide them with all the information, they can sell themselves.*

Listener's Observation. *The presenter gave us a lot of information, but it was not very compelling. It felt like this was a class or a lecture.*

Solution. Get Clear on the Goal of Being Persuasive

It is a teacher's job to be informative. It is a sales professional's job to be persuasive. When crafting your persuasive message, it is vital to understand that difference. Sales professionals are not unbiased. Their goal is to promote a specific point of view, opportunity, or way of thinking or acting. By design, sales professionals have intent and build arguments for why clients should work with them and their companies, and why working together is beneficial to the listener. Crafting a persuasive presentation can be challenging, but it is not impossible. It is a skill you can master.

Three Presentation Categories

There are three kinds of presentations: informative, ceremonial, and persuasive.

> ▶ **Informative.** An informative presentation is objective. It is unbiased and promotes learning; it is cooperative rather than competitive. In an informative presentation, there is no action for the audience to take. The presenter's intention is merely to educate. For example, if you've been tapped to present the findings of a research paper at a university banquet, your purpose is to inform the audience about the project, its key discoveries, and the results. Informative presentations promote audience

understanding and foster cooperation by presenting a subject matter in an unbiased way.

▶ **Ceremonial.** A ceremonial presentation appeals to values that are cherished by a group, and its intention is to provide a sense of communion with the audience. For example, it could be the toast made at a wedding by the best man or the lifetime achievement award acceptance speech at the Golden Globes. It is appropriate at a social gathering, a celebration, or a memorial.

▶ **Persuasive.** A persuasive presentation, by design, has a specific intention. The speaker wants the listeners to act based on what they are hearing. This presentation is typically a transactional process and should provide choices to the listeners without duress. For example, if you are a sales professional for a cosmetics company speaking to a group of prospects, you will introduce yourself, explain why your product line is unique compared with your competitor's, and state how the prospects can benefit and ultimately buy the products directly from you today.

When choosing from these three options, too many business professionals migrate toward the informative presentation any time they are meeting with clients and prospects. Instead of delivering a persuasive talk, they give an informative one. The informative speech or presentation is rarely the salesperson's best option because the reality is that the data-dump syndrome is a common pitfall and does not motivate a listener to take action.

SCENARIO 2

Presenter's Confession. *I gave them a lot of information. I didn't want to be hard sell or pushy, but I think I need a better strategy to be both persuasive and informative.*

Listener's Observation. *Wow, that was a total data dump and too technical. They told us they were "creative problem solvers." At the very least, I was hoping for some clarity about how to best move forward. They just sounded like everyone else we have been talking to.*

Solution. Craft Your Message Using a Persuasive Formula with Clear Arguments and Unique Talking Points

Imagine a courtroom. The judge is at the front, and prosecutor and defense attorneys are ready to address the jury. When the gavel hits the desk and the trial begins, the attorneys stand up and begin to present their *opening arguments*. Then they introduce the evidence, testimony, witnesses, and so on—and provide the court with the material supporting the arguments they made at the beginning of their case. When their presentation of evidence and testimony is over, they end with *closing arguments*. Their cases are carefully crafted to reflect a balance between the persuasive and the informative.

Similarly, sales professionals can benefit greatly from remembering that their goal is to argue one or multiple points before their listeners to reach a specific conclusion or outcome.

One of the simplest and most effective methods of communicating a persuasive message with the right balance of information is found in the work of Alan H. Monroe, a professor at Purdue University in the 1930s. In the tenth edition of the much-used textbook *Principles and Types of Speech Communication*, we learn that Monroe united two sets of procedures: "One set based on the personalized scientific method, and the other rooted in an understanding of human motivation—to form a highly useful organizational pattern. . . . It is simultaneously problem-solution oriented and motivation-centered."

His formula, commonly known as Monroe's Motivated Sequence, is based on a clean, logical progression, not crazy or manipulative closing tactics. As the name suggests, this pattern is based on the normal, sequential processes of human thinking that motivate an audience to respond affirmatively to a presenter's purpose. In simple terms, this means that most people, when presented with a clear challenge, will naturally shift into a problem-solving mode. The textbook says, "The Motivated Sequence is a time tested and flexible organizational pattern, one based on a speaker's two fundamental communicative concerns: a concern for creative problem solving and a concern for the audience's motives."

The sequence contains five distinct steps: attention, need, satisfaction, visualization, and action. Each step plays a vital role in shaping and crafting a persuasive message.

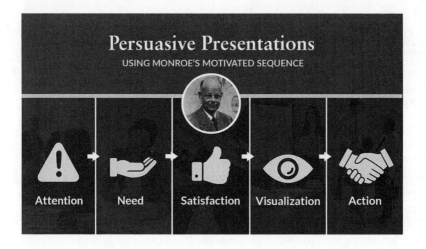

1. **Attention Step.** Create an awakening in the mind of your listeners. Gain their attention in a favorable way by sharing information that will give them a reason to sit up and listen. Aim to spark curiosity and leave them open to exploring a new path.
2. **Need Step.** Help your listeners feel a need for change to solve a problem. Monroe suggests, "The psychological center of the Motivated Sequence is the Need Step—using motivational appeals together with solid evidence to stir the minds and feelings of the listener." Simply put, why do they need you?

People approach challenges with different levels of awareness about what they need or what they can do to solve a problem. Depending on how much they know, we may have to help them out. How many times have you ever worked with people who did not know what they needed or how you could help?

3. **Satisfaction Step.** After you inspire a sense of need, satisfy it by providing a solution to the problem. Show your listeners specifically *how* your company, product, service, or plan can work to solve an issue or challenge. Support your arguments as introduced in the Need Step with strong evidence.

4. **Visualization Step.** Invite the audience to imagine themselves in the future, enjoying the benefits that follow the adoption of your plan. Help prospects visualize change. Take them from their present condition to the enhanced lifestyle they envision for themselves. Unless they can see themselves moving into a new dimension, they won't be convinced that your offering is necessary.

5. **Action Step.** Encourage your listeners to take action, perhaps by signing an agreement or setting up the next appointment time. Briefly explain what *you* will do once they have made a choice to move forward. What comes next? When you develop the earlier part of your presentation in a convincing way, the close, or call to action, is a natural part of the process to keep things moving forward.

Monroe and his coauthors explain, "The Motivated Sequence has its own internal logic aimed at satisfying audience questions: attention precedes need; need precedes satisfaction; and so on." As you outline your presentation, you should clearly note this sense of progression that the message must have for a listener to feel comfortable about moving forward. This is based on the natural processes of human thinking.

To further explore solutions under the mistake of being too informative versus persuasive, we are looking specifically at the Need Step in Monroe's sequence in this chapter. We will address the material and content relating to each of the other steps in later sections of the book.

Identifying Needs and Crafting Unique Arguments and Talking Points

If you want to figure out your listeners' needs, spend some time thinking about all the problems decision makers face. They may realize that they could use an offering like yours but lack sufficient motivation to buy it. In the process, if they do decide to buy, will they shop other providers? If so, will they return to you because you are the best fit for them?

In the past, the answer was to provide a grocery list of features and benefits to listeners. Selling on features and benefits alone is more difficult today, and it's not compelling. In competitive markets, people purchase what they feel they need or what they really want. Unfortunately, a stand-alone features-and-benefits presentation rarely brings a strong sense of urgency. A presenter must identify listeners' needs and craft situation-specific arguments to help prospects understand why they should consider buying your solution.

Passing the "So What?" Test

One vital tool for crafting a persuasive presentation is running your arguments through the "so what?" test. The easiest way to explain the "so what?" test is to put it into practice. Take Paul, for example. Paul has great contacts and sells advertising for an impressive and growing online magazine. When meeting with prospects, he likes to underscore that his company is number one in the space. His company also has the largest reader base in

MISTAKE #2: BEING OVERLY INFORMATIVE VERSUS PERSUASIVE **25**

the market and the lowest ad rates. But those accolades haven't turned up many clients. Paul's problem is that simply saying his company is number one doesn't make it pass the "so what?" test for his clients.

Things that pass the "so what?" test typically focus on matters that keep people up at night. Salespeople often say, "Our company is number one!," "We really care!," "We're the biggest!," and "We provide a lot of choices!" So what? What does that mean to me? People aren't lying in bed at night thinking, "If only they were number one!," "If only they cared!," or "If only they offered more choices!"

Paul and other sales professionals must show clients how their companies are poised to meet or exceed clients' needs. Paul says his online magazine is more popular than any other. So what? Many people use these descriptions, but they don't translate into anything real for Paul's prospects. A compelling argument is more specific. For example, a prospect wants to know how many more hourly hits he will receive on Paul's site than on his competitor's site and how that will translate to sales. Paul can say his site has the latest security protections. So what? His prospect wants to know what measures are in place to ensure data safety.

Quite simply, a speaker's case, argument, or presentation must answer the following question for the listener: What does this mean to me? Superlatives—"best," "largest," "oldest," "newest," "most popular"—are wonderful in ceremonial speeches. They are less helpful when trying to persuade an audience or trying to convince listeners that they need what you are offering—unless you can prove it! All prospects have their own set of specific needs and preferences. They may not even know that a solution exists until you tell them. Practice using this bridge line: "What this means to you is . . ." You might have some really good ideas that just need to be refined. When you make a statement, ask yourself, "What does this mean for the listener?" If the answer is "not much," the statement doesn't pass the "so what?" test.

26 PRESENTATION READY

The takeaway: How you finish the statement, "What this means to you is . . ." is gold. This exercise helps you think about the core of what will most likely be your next argument or selling point for the listener. Example: What this means to you is that we can save you _____ when we do _____ .

Six General Case Arguments That Work

Another effective way to develop a compelling case is to employ proven arguments that have impact. Consider these examples, which may or may not apply to your particular industry and audience. They will help you think about arguments you can customize for your own situation. These six arguments have been field-tested and reflect what our research has shown about how to move listeners toward action based on what *they* want and need:

1. **Time.** How will you save them time? Your prospects don't care if you are the oldest company in your field. They want to know how your methods and processes are going to save their organizations and their people time each day. What would time savings mean to their productivity?
2. **Money.** How will you save them money? They don't care if you are the largest company around. They want to spend less with your company than they would with a competitor and be in a better position than they are now.
3. **Sanity.** How are you going to save them mental sanity or put their situation in better order? Your prospects don't care if you are the best in your field unless you can show them specifically how you can provide effective solutions to existing problems and eliminate "crazy-making" stressful issues.
4. **Security.** How are you going to provide them with a sense of security? They don't care if you have been around for 200 years. Will you be here tomorrow? They need to know that partnering

MISTAKE #2: BEING OVERLY INFORMATIVE VERSUS PERSUASIVE **27**

with you is a safe decision. Safety, security, and solvency all live in this argument.

5. **Fun.** How are you going to help them have fun? They don't want to work with people who have dronelike personalities. They want to know that doing business with you will be an enjoyable experience.

6. **Ease of use.** How will you make things easy? Your prospects don't care that your product uses the latest and greatest technological advances. If it's too complicated or confusing to use, they won't see any advantage in owning it.

Each of the above arguments meets the requirements in the Need Step in Monroe's Motivated Sequence.

> *Note* *Everybody sells something, whether it's a product, a service, a philosophy, or an idea. It is possible to sell and be persuasive in a very elegant, polished manner without being overly informative.*

Consider Mary, a midlevel sales associate at a successful financial services firm, who had just experienced the most brutal week of her career. On Monday morning she was optimistic, excited about having multiple in-person appointments and videoconferencing meetings on the books and a handful of promising leads. By late Friday afternoon, however, Mary was dejected. Although she felt the meetings had gone well, she had accomplished no conversions at all—no signed contracts and no next appointment times. She shared her disappointment with her vice president of sales, who asked her how long the meetings were taking, how she was closing, and the prospects' response. Mary acknowledged that she felt most comfortable in the information zone, and as a result, her strategy was simply to provide more information than her competitor did. She hoped that her prospects would like her more or at least feel obligated to buy because she had been so thorough. The more Mary examined her presentations, the more she realized that she was a data dumper. She needed to move beyond merely relaying information to building a solid case. By focusing on brevity and tailoring her strongest points to her prospects' needs, Mary eventually became a consistent producer in her organization.

Your goal is to be both informative and persuasive, pairing rock-solid information with compelling arguments. If you are too informative, nothing happens. If you are too aggressive, nothing happens. Find a balance, and you will see results.

Summary

Mistake #2 is being overly informative versus persuasive by overloading a presentation with an excessive amount of information—often without the proper context or explanation, failing to balance facts and data with an effective argument or point.

- This is ranked as one of the most common mistakes that professionals self-confess to making when presenting, whether the meeting is in person, virtual, or hybrid.

- There are three presentation types or categories—informative, persuasive, and ceremonial. If you are on a job interview, it's a persuasive talk; you want them to hire you! Sales presentations fall under the category of persuasive.

- Many sales professionals tend to linger in the information zone, citing features and benefits, and delay getting into the persuasive zone. Either they are not persuasive enough, or they save the persuasive material until the very end when it is often too late. The customer often has little desire to make a buying decision following a predominantly informative presentation.

- Monroe's Motivated Sequence is an effective method of communicating a persuasive message with the right balance of information. The sequence contains five distinct steps—attention, need, satisfaction, visualization, and action—and each step plays a vital role in shaping and crafting a persuasive message.

- Monroe's Motivated Sequence encourages the speaker to build on solid arguments throughout the entire talk. It also puts less pressure on speakers as they approach the close, which makes the "ask" easier.

- Make sure your arguments pass the "so what?" test by following up with, "What this means to you is . . ." Be sure your arguments are poised to solve a specific issue or concern.

▶ **Next Up.** Mistake #3: Providing Inadequate Support

MISTAKE #3

Providing Inadequate Support

DEFINITION
Lacking sufficient credible material assistance, facts, or other information to substantiate your claims. An absence of quality evidence paired with thoughtful analysis to support your proposition.

Understanding the Issue of Providing Inadequate Support

Presenters who move listeners to act know the importance of providing undeniable social proof and evidence for their claims. Better still, evidence that has a *wow* factor can make a yes-let's-move-forward decision much easier for the listener. Decision makers want measurable performance, quantified improvement, and comparable value. They are seeking proof of what you, your product, or your service can do for them to make them feel comfortable with taking action based on your presentation.

To avoid committing the mistake of providing inadequate support, it is helpful to look back at the Satisfaction Step of Monroe's Motivated Sequence. In this step, a speaker supports the ideas shared in the Need Step by showing the listeners how their company, product, service, or plan can solve a problem. We asked you to practice saying, "What this means to you is . . ." because that statement serves as the bridge line connecting the ideas of the Need Step to the Satisfaction Step where you provide the necessary support. It's the moment you explain to listeners exactly how you will save them time, money, sanity, and security, pairing your arguments with carefully crafted social and scientific proof.

This mistake of providing inadequate support can also be tied to data dumping, with the difference being that the presenter's job is about "sense-making." It's up to the presenter to make sense of the data, giving it meaning by articulating exactly how the data validates a recommended solution for the listener. Avoiding this mistake requires presenters to rely on logic, reason, and facts rather than anecdotes, humor, or charm.

In recent years, there has been a trend in the market to focus on "selling the story." This approach is effective and fun, but it can lead some speakers to fall into the trap of all sizzle and no substance. It's only when speakers pair rock-solid evidence with a compelling story that they present a balanced case. We saw this demonstrated clearly in our research study. The results showed that sales professionals who committed the mistake of providing inadequate support consistently:

- ▶ Failed to establish credibility with the listener through their personal experience or data quality
- ▶ Relied too much on storytelling with little supporting evidence
- ▶ Provided inadequate, irrelevant, or outdated evidence and support

Real-World Confessions

We asked our study participants to share their experiences and observations as both listeners and presenters. They revealed valuable dual insights not only from their own presentations, but also from their colleagues' talks. Providing inadequate support is the presentation mistake most likely to have a negative effect on a listener wanting to work with that specific presenter, and on a listener moving forward with an entire company. Study participants said they had seen this mistake play out in a variety of ways. Some of these instances were subtle, generating just enough unease to discourage listeners from moving forward, while others were glaringly obvious and almost immediately off-putting. Examples ranged from speakers using outdated material, to providing irrelevant information, to lying outright about a product's benefits.

As with any mistake, to avoid making it, one must understand how it manifests in the real world. Let's explore what some of our research participants said about providing inadequate support.

SCENARIO 1

Presenter's Confession. *I realize that because I'm new to the industry, I need to focus more on the credibility and value of my data, and less about me as a resource and my personal experience.*

Listener's Observation. *This kid was green, a newbie to the industry. Their knowledge of their own product was limited, and they did not demonstrate a clear understanding of our company's needs. They were way out of their league trying to convince us they could handle this project.*

Solution. Establish Your Credibility as a Presenter and Demonstrate the Quality of Your Material to Be More Persuasive

As mentioned earlier, to earn a potential client's confidence or trust, it's necessary to be highly credible and to build a case that meets the client's specific needs. So how do you do that? Look at credibility from two perspectives: your personal credibility and the credibility of your content.

Achieving Credibility

Most sales professionals like to think of themselves as trustworthy and believable, but the undeniable profit they receive from convincing someone to buy can make them suspect in the eyes of a listener. Sales is a profession with a history that includes plenty of examples of ethical breaches, so you can understand why it is terribly important to establish credibility. In their book *Credibility: How Leaders Gain and Lose It, and Why People Demand It*, authors James M. Kouzes and Barry Z. Posner write, "Credibility is mostly about the consistency between words and deeds. People listen to the words and look at the deeds. They measure the congruence. A judgment of 'credible' is handed down when the two are consonant." When you make a presentation, you implicitly commit to a variety of things, from showing up on time to delivering the mutually agreed content. When a presentation is full of vague assertions and imprecise data, you lose credibility. Without a persuasive case, a prospect does not have the confidence to buy into your proposal.

A potential customer will evaluate you and your information before deciding whether to believe you. Personal credibility speaks to your experience, education, background, industry knowledge, and field work. If you are new to an industry, it's tough to sell your experience. Your chances are better if you sell your work ethic and scrappy mindset instead of your ability to advise listeners on how to do something they have been doing for the past 20 years. In this situation, you must lean on the experience of others within your company or trusted mentors until you can build up your own track record of experience and knowledge.

Whether you are a novice or veteran in your industry, establishing your credibility as a presenter is vital. If your prospects do not believe in you or what you are saying, convincing them to buy what you are selling will be virtually impossible.

Side note: Somebody once asked, "What is the most difficult product or service to sell?" The answer is simple: The one you don't believe in. If you do not fully believe in what you are selling or the service you represent, it will become apparent to your listeners and ultimately undermine all your efforts. Your feelings and personal confidence must be aligned with your message to help establish personal credibility.

SCENARIO 2

Presenter's Confession. *My data was a little light, but I thought the examples I gave would be enough. I relied too heavily on my long-term relationship with the listener, without building a new case for why they should continue to work with me in the future.*

Listener's Observation. *I really like working with this person, and have worked with them for years, but that's not enough to continue with this relationship in today's market. Their pitch was all story and conjecture with no proof. Too much fluff and not enough substance to make the new team feel good about moving forward.*

Solution. Provide Supporting Evidence with Your Storytelling to Create a Balanced Message

Opinion and storytelling might speak to a person's heart, but that alone is not enough in most cases to convince listeners to act. Speakers must support what they say with a variety of facts that appeal to their listeners' minds. While a speaker's opinion is valuable and certainly has a place in any persuasive presentation, hard data and your analysis of that data provide the foundation for the overall case. Many presenters say, "The data

Evidence works well when paired with storytelling to create balance.

speaks for itself," but the reality is the data has no voice. You are the voice of the data.

This mistake is often noted by seasoned professionals for why they lost a long-standing client to a competitor. They don't keep showing the return on investment or the advancement of their company's capabilities in the same way that a competitor would.

SCENARIO 3

Presenter's Confession. *Looking back, I realized I gave more of a grocery list of what my product could do, but I didn't do a good job of proving that we can do what I said we can do. I didn't share any of our latest research or results from happy clients. A lot of the research in our existing slide deck is a bit dated.*

Listener's Observation. *The presenter gave us an overview of what they can do but didn't have any evidence to support his claims. We have been working in this industry for more than 20 years, and his examples were old. How can they take us to the next level if they are stuck in the past?*

Solution. Provide Social Proof and/or Scientific Evidence in the Form of Relevant Studies, Research Data, Customer Testimonials, Surveys, Documentary Videos and Instructional Films, and Demonstrations

With the large amount of information now available to the public on the internet, listeners are better informed than ever before. They can differentiate between your product or service and that of your competitors with a few keystrokes, whether they are at their desks or on their phones. Get ahead of the game and be their go-to source for fact-based information.

Effective Presentation Supports to Help Prove Your Case

Let's briefly discuss a few presentation supports to consider as you are building the evidence for your talking points:

- ▶ Relevant studies, data, and statistics
- ▶ Testimonials (trusted opinions from people with similar needs)
- ▶ Personalized surveys (polls and case studies with timely results from a relevant audience)
- ▶ Documentary videos and instructional films
- ▶ Demonstrations

Relevant Studies, Data, and Statistics

Statistics is the branch of mathematics that lets us organize and interpret numerical data. A good statistic, followed up by an interesting anecdote or testimonial, will make a strong impression if you can draw a direct correlation between your data and your talking point. The impact depends on how dramatic the numbers are. Too many statistics will put your audience to sleep. Remember, data is supposed to tell listeners whether a future bet is sound and that their choice to move forward is a wise one.

Testimonials (Trusted Opinions from People with Similar Needs)

A testimonial is a formal recommendation, made by someone who has reason to know what they're talking about. By incorporating testimonials into a presentation, you reinforce your claims with the weight of another person's reputation—and their proven credibility.

A testimonial says, "Look, these people were feeling concerned, just as you are," or "These people had doubts, just as you do. They moved forward

38 PRESENTATION READY

and got the outcome they were hoping for. Now they are thrilled to provide a testimonial about their experience."

Personalized Surveys (Polls and Case Studies with Timely Results from a Relevant Audience)

From simple online survey queries to internal questionnaires, client case studies can capture a snapshot of audience opinion, knowledge, background, and feelings within defined parameters. This information provides a unique perspective that can be quite compelling as a source of social proof for your talking points.

Documentary Videos and Instructional Films

Seeing is believing. When a presenter shares a video, film, or visual experience that shows how a specific product or service works, it is incredibly powerful.

Demonstrations

Nothing beats showing someone how something works. Instead of telling your audience, show them in real time, in person. When they can engage with the product—touch, feel, smell, see, or taste—and experience the results, it is easier to visualize how they can use the product or service in their day-to-day life and activities.

Blending Support and Passion

Many sales professionals argue that people don't want to hear a presentation with too much data, because data is boring. While that's a given, listeners also don't want to sit through a presentation with too little evidence. What most decision makers want is the right balance of facts and figures with stories and opinions. When presenters achieve this balance,

MISTAKE #3: PROVIDING INADEQUATE SUPPORT   **39**

they successfully blend their product's overarching story with its concrete capabilities. That pairing is a winning combination.

We see a classic example of using numbers and data to craft a compelling message in one of President Harry S. Truman's famed Whistlestop speeches. In one given on September 18, 1948, in Chariton, Iowa, "Give 'em Hell" Harry used numbers and statistics to open his audience's eyes to his arguments. Here's some of what he told folks that day: "In 1932, 123,000 farmers in the United States had lost their farms. In 1947, less than 800 farms were foreclosed."

That was one of the most dramatic reductions in farm foreclosures in history.

"In 1932, the farmers were hopelessly in debt," Truman continued. "Their indebtedness has been reduced by more than 50 percent and they have $18 billion in assets. Think of that! Just think of that!"

Truman went on to warn his audience that the opposing party wanted to reverse that prosperity, do away with price-support programs for farmers, and "turn the clock back to the horse-and-buggy days with such people that made up the 'do-nothing' 80th Congress."

He then placed the solution to the problem squarely in the hands of his audience. "That Congress tried its level best to take all the rights away from labor . . . to put the farmer back to 1932 . . . to put small business out of business. . . . You stayed at home in 1946, and you got the 80th Congress, and you got just exactly what you deserved. You didn't exercise your God-given right to control this country. Now you're going to have another chance. If you let that chance slip, you won't have my sympathy. If you don't let that chance slip, you'll do me a very great favor, for I'll live in the White House another 4 years."

And he did. The strategy worked. Truman was reelected on November 2, 1948.

Granted, he was the sitting president, and not everyone can be as aggressive as he was that day. You can still take a cue from his passion and certainty and, of course, his use of numbers and statistics.

Summary

Mistake #3 is providing inadequate support. It happens when speakers lack sufficient credible material assistance, facts, or other information to substantiate their claims.

- Listeners want measured performance, quantified improvement, and compared value.

- When a presentation is filled with vague assertions and imprecise data, speakers lose credibility. Credibility is essential. Without it, a prospect has little reason to buy into your proposal.

- It's only when speakers pair rock-solid evidence and key talking points with compelling stories that they present a balanced case.

- Remember that the data does not speak for itself. You are the voice of the data.

- Use effective presentation supports—relevant studies, and research data, customer testimonials, personalized surveys, documentary videos and instructional films, and demonstrations—to build the evidence for your talking points.

▶ **Next Up.** Mistake #4: Failing to Close the Sale

MISTAKE #4

Failing to Close the Sale

DEFINITION
Neglecting to ask the listener to complete a transaction or take some sort of "Action Step" in response to your message and/or proposition. Failure to motivate the listener to move forward in the professional relationship.

Understanding the Issue of Failing to Close the Sale

In the State of Sales Presentations research study, failing to close the sale was one of the top three most common presentation mistakes that participants reported committing.

Many individuals reluctantly confessed that they conclude but do not close. The close is the specific call to action you want your listener to take after hearing your message. A conclusion is a wrap-up of what you just said. Some people avoid closing altogether because they don't want to risk hearing "no thanks, not interested." The fear of rejection makes closing feel uncomfortable, so they just skip it altogether.

It doesn't need to be scary. All you are doing is inviting your listener to choose to move forward in some regard. In many situations, people will do exactly what they are inspired to do. But when it comes to parting with hard-earned money, it's almost guaranteed that they won't do anything until they are asked to do so.

42 PRESENTATION READY

Delivering a persuasive presentation requires the ability to close. Persuasive presenters are always prepared to ask for a next step, or commitment—it's what they're there to do. If you have met with numerous prospects but haven't completed many transactions, ask yourself, "Do I close, or do I conclude?" One generates action; the other gives your prospect the option of doing nothing.

A Few Real-World Confessions

We asked our study participants to share their experiences and observations as both listeners and presenters. They revealed not only what they said during their own presentations, but also what they heard and witnessed in their colleagues' talks, providing valuable dual insights about what constitutes a successful persuasive presentation. The results showed that sales professionals who committed the mistake of failing to close the sale also consistently failed to (1) decide on the specific goal with a clear call to action for that meeting and (2) ask the listener to set up the next appointment time when it was clear the prospect was not ready to make a commitment. (This is a pivot strategy.)

When presenters fail to close, it's often because they psych themselves out by thinking about the close as some hugely complex add-on to their talk. It's not an add-on. It's simply the natural next step in the progression of a persuasive presentation. The close is the necessary culmination of the Action Step in Monroe's Motivated Sequence. You ask for what you want—the meeting, the sale, the endorsement, the contribution—and explain the next steps to your listener. Within that explanation, you map out exactly what will take place after the listener agrees to partner with you or your organization. As you fulfill the Action Step, it's important to stay in a consultative headspace so that your call to action is based not only on what you want, but on what you want to make happen for your prospect. It should feel like a win-win.

As with any mistake, to avoid making it, we must understand how it manifests in the real world. Let's explore what some of our participants say about being concluders instead of closers.

SCENARIO 1

Presenter's Confession. *I'm good at talking about our service, but I hate to close, so I avoid doing it. I don't want to be hard sell.*

Listener's Observation. *Very informative presentation. Just no clear path forward. I wasn't sure what the next step would be. The inspiration to say yes today wasn't there. I'd like to think about it.*

Solution. Decide on the Specific Goal with a Clear Call to Action for That Meeting

One effective way to avoid this mistake is to understand the role of the close in a persuasive presentation. The close is the point at which you bring the two-part Action Step of Monroe's Motivated Sequence to life by transitioning the desire created in the Visualization Step into action.

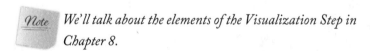

We'll talk about the elements of the Visualization Step in Chapter 8.

- ▶ **Part one of the Action Step: Make your offer of service.** State what you want to happen as a result of your meeting or presentation. For example, "It's my goal to learn more about your needs and how I might be of service to your company so that we can work together in some capacity long term." This serves as a soft transition to your close.

- ▶ **Part two of the Action Step: Identify your specific "ask" for this meeting or appointment.** In your close, ask for the next step in the process: whether it is to set up the next appointment time, sign an agreement, request an introduction, or take whatever other Action Step will keep the relationship progressing.

While most sales professionals would prefer closing to be a one-and-done moment, in reality it's often a far more fluid experience. Sometimes it can take several presentations to complete a single transaction. It's not unusual to have to make several presentations if a big investment of time or resources is on the line, if it's a complex sale, or if multiple people must weigh in on the decision.

The same can be true for job hunters or those seeking a promotion. It's not uncommon to have four, five, or even six interviews before receiving an official offer. Maybe multiple people must meet and approve of you before you can come aboard. In each interview, it's helpful to have a clear objective in mind of what is needed to take the next step in the interview process.

Closing an Interoffice Presentation

A reluctance to close has significant consequences in the business world. Sometimes even in interoffice meetings, when we are required to get together to discuss certain things that are happening, many of the meetings end up being informational. And there is work to be done! What's frustrating is that frequently there are no action steps defined following a presentation in an internal meeting. That can be the reason it takes so long to get things done. An effective leadership-based close for an interoffice meeting would be to ask, *What are the Action Steps we must take now? What do we want to happen next because of this meeting?* With those questions clearly on the table, every participant is aware of the objective and able to offer an appropriate response.

SCENARIO 2

Presenter's Confession. *I wrapped up the meeting and asked the prospects if they had any questions, and they said no, thanked me, and assured me they'd think about it. I told them I'd follow up with them in a day or two and sent an email outlining the costs. I also called and left a message but never heard back from them, and now I realize this is happening a bit too often.*

Listener's Observation. *I was interested, but I wasn't ready to decide. I needed to pull in a couple of other people before I could move forward.*

Solution. If a Prospective Client Is Not Ready to Make a Commitment, Use a Pivot Strategy—Ask the Client to Set up a Next Appointment Time

No matter how good you sound or how persuasive your case is, you will run into situations where people say, "I would like to think about it." Nothing works every time, but here is a solution you can put into your tool bag in case a situation like this comes up.

When you get to the close, ask the listener to make a commitment or move forward. If the person says, "You know what, I'd like to think about it," you can respond, with "Okay, I understand this is a big decision and you may want to review some of the materials I've given you. I know you are very busy, so let's do this. Why don't we break out our calendars right now and set up the next appointment time when we can get together? I'm sure that once you have had an opportunity to review the content and the agreement I've prepared for you, you will have several questions. I can answer them for you during our visit, whether we meet in person or via videoconference."

 Note *Our research study showed that a higher percentage of people fail to close the sale via videoconference than at in-person presentations. So keep this in mind when you are presenting virtually.*

The first reason to use the pivot strategy option is that it helps you avoid feeling like a nuisance. Maybe you can relate to this! When you try repeatedly to follow up with a client, leaving several unreturned messages, you don't want to call anymore. Having to push those boundaries is uncomfortable, and it's tempting to simply let go of the prospect and assume the sale is dead.

If your listeners are hesitant about setting up the next appointment time, try to arrange it at a place that is attractive to them: a nice restaurant of their choosing or perhaps a golf course. Think of it as just another way to incentivize them to meet with you and keep the transaction moving forward.

Most people are amenable to setting up the next appointment. If they continue to balk, chances are their refusal may reveal their real objection. When you can find out what that objection is, you can work to overcome it.

A Bit of Pushback

I Know I Need to Close, but I Do Not Want to Be Perceived as Pushy

It's kind of ironic: Some sales professionals are accused of being "hard sell," even when many aren't closing at all. When the moment arrives, they commit a wide range of missteps that include talking around their close, talking too much, or just thanking the listeners for their time and saying, "If you have any questions or want to move forward, call me."

"Call me" is not a close. Some presenters balk at the close because they feel that final ask is clumsy and clunky, and they're worried about being seen as pushy. But the close doesn't have to be any of those things. It's fully appropriate and supposed to happen in a persuasive presentation.

The close is a vital part of any transaction and can be completed elegantly. It only requires a bit of finesse. In fact, most prospects expect it. When a presenter skips the close, the omission is noticeable, and listeners are at times left wondering what's next. They are much less likely to act than if they had heard your close or "ask." People are not surprised when you wrap up your meeting with a clear call to action. They know that's why you're there. When you skip it, you get in your own way.

> If there is something to gain and nothing
> to lose by asking, by all means—ask!
> —W. CLEMENT STONE

The Elevator Story

Consider the story of a young man vying for a new marketing and sales manager position. Following two preliminary videoconference interviews, he is invited to a third interview, this time in person with the company vice president. After they talk for a while, the vice president asks the candidate if he has any questions. The young man declines, says he understands what the job entails, and thanks the vice president for his time. Then he asks, "Do you know when you will make a final decision about hiring someone?" The vice president says that they want to think about it. He will hear back, one way or the other, within two weeks.

The young man thanks him and walks out of the office. Once in the hallway, he realizes he never actually asked the vice president for the job. Knowing the importance of closing, the young man mentally berates himself, wishing he could walk back inside and have a do-over. He then makes a quick trip to the restroom before heading back to the hallway to summon an elevator. He realizes the man directly in front of him is the company vice president who just interviewed him. They exchange an awkward greeting and step into the elevator.

The young man decides he isn't going to miss another opportunity. He looks the vice president in the eye and says, "You know, sir, as I walked out of the interview, I thought to myself that the one thing I didn't tell you was how much I want this job." He uses the next few moments to emphasize how much he wants the position, how much research he has done on the company, and how inappropriate it was to apply for a sales-related job

48 PRESENTATION READY

and not close at the end of the visit. Finally he says, "I would really like an opportunity to be a part of your team. When you are thinking about whom you are going to select, I really hope you will consider me. More importantly, I want to let you know that I very much want this job."

The vice president smiles and says, "You know what, young man, nice recovery. Because you have asked for it, it's yours. I'll have the HR department process your paperwork. Let's get you on board!" That's a small message with a big impact and a literal "elevator speech"!

Meanwhile the young man is beyond excited. He walks off the elevator in a daze, looks up at the sky, and says, "Thank you." Then he congratulates himself, knowing that if he hadn't asked for the job, he wouldn't have been offered it. He was so lucky to get a second chance. But was it simply luck? As the saying goes, "Luck is when preparation meets opportunity."

Summary

Mistake #4 is failing to close the sale: neglecting to ask the listener to complete a transaction or take some sort of action in response to a presentation.

- A conclusion is a wrap-up. A close is the specific call to action: what you want your listeners to do as a result of your talk.

- Fear of rejection is a common reason people avoid closing. Remember: You don't get what you don't ask for, and your competitor will most likely ask if you don't.

- The close is the necessary culmination of the Action Step in Monroe's Motivated Sequence.

- Decide on a specific goal with a clear call to action for the listeners at your meeting.

- If a prospective client is not ready to make a commitment, it's appropriate to use a pivot strategy and ask the client to set up a next appointment time.

▶ **Next Up.** Mistake #5: Misusing the Allotted Time

SECTION II
CREATIVITY

Creativity addresses how your persuasive message resonates with listeners. It relies on storytelling, visual aids, structure, curiosity, and the way you customize your language to meet your audience's needs.

MISTAKE #5

Misusing the Allotted Time

DEFINITION
Ineffectively using the time allotted for a presentation, resulting in a critical imbalance of content. This could include running out of time to make key points, spending too little time on key points, or simply lacking an awareness of the time you have been allotted.

Understanding the Issue of Misusing the Allotted Time

Now that you understand how to best develop the case of your message, let's focus on the creative elements of a presentation, so that it will land squarely in the hearts and minds of an audience, beginning with how to best use the amount of time you have to speak. Most prospects and listeners are juggling packed schedules, and they expect presenters to work within their time constraints.

Avoiding this mistake is especially important today, as an increasing number of sales calls continue to move onto videoconference platforms for reasons of cost savings, time savings, and simple convenience. When delivering in-person presentations, it's easier for speakers to adapt to time constraints, and there's wiggle room to ease in and out of a meeting. That is often not the case in an online setting. Many companies schedule videoconferencing meetings very close together to maximize time use, and when the clock strikes, speakers face the unforgiving "hard stop." You can be left trying to manage an abrupt ending when things are finally getting rolling or even find yourself staring at an empty screen while still waiting to close—and that's not a good feeling.

For today's presenters, the challenge is understanding and honoring the time allotment they are given while still effectively communicating what they want to say. Without careful planning, your talk can end up being too short, too long, or just horribly lopsided. Although most sales professionals believe they have a decent sense of timing and the ability to read the room in a meeting or presentation, it's still remarkably easy to misuse the allotted time.

In the State of Sales Presentations research study, research participants frequently reported this mistake as something they saw others commit, but not as a mistake they often made themselves. When people watch a playback of their own presentations, however, they recognize this mistake in their own work more often. A confession of "Yeah, I could really have used my time better" is a typical response.

A Few Real-World Confessions

Our study results showed that sales professionals who misused their allotted time consistently failed to:

- ▶ Get clear on how much time they had to share their message
- ▶ Prepare an outline to provide an effective structure and manage content
- ▶ Use the time they had been given effectively

As with any mistake, to avoid making it, one must understand how it manifests in the real world. Let's explore what some of our research participants have said about this topic.

SCENARIO 1

Presenter's Confession. *I thought we were going to meet for an hour, but once I got into the meeting, they told me we had 30 minutes, so I had to adjust my presentation in the moment. When I realized I was running out of time, I rushed through the second part of my talk, and the whole thing was lopsided. The client had to leave, and I was not able to cover all the key information.*

Listener's Observation. *We felt bad because we had to cut the meeting short, and it seemed to really throw them off and they couldn't adapt. It just didn't go well. The speaker had some interesting ideas, but we had a hard stop, and they seemed to rush through their talking points at the end.*

Solution. Clarify Your Time Allotment

One simple, straightforward strategy is plainly asking the listener how much time you have been given to meet or present. At the start of a virtual meeting, in-person visit, or telephone call, it's entirely appropriate to clarify any time limits, not only to respect your prospect's schedule but also to ensure that you handle your time parameters effectively. This can be especially helpful if you are required to edit down your message on the fly due to last-minute time constraints.

Typically, before a scheduled meeting, we have some idea of how much time we will have to present. An average in-person meeting lasts about an hour. According to Zoom, an average video call lasts between 31 and 60 minutes.

During either an in-person or online appointment, you will need to spend a few minutes at the start building rapport, devote 20 to 30 minutes to your actual presentation, and use a few minutes at the end for a graceful exit. That said, each meeting opportunity is unique, and sometimes that time gets cut short.

Do the Math

When that meeting—whether 30 minutes or 3 minutes—you've worked for finally comes along, you must be able to balance your content across the time allotted. It helps to approach your presentation outline like a math equation. Recall the basic structure of any presentation: an introduction that grabs the listener's attention, a body made up of three main points, a conclusion, and a close. That's a total of six components. Let's say you have 30 minutes to speak. To balance your content, divide the total number of minutes by the six components:

30 minutes ÷ 6 components = 5 minutes per section

By adhering to this mathematical breakdown, you can exert control over the clock and fight the urge to panic. (The amount of time per segment doesn't have to be identical. This equation simply serves as a guideline to help balance the talking points in your message.)

A sales meeting is not a monologue. You never know if you will be asked to expand on a particular topic of interest or to cut down your talk because a decision maker has to leave. Consider this analogy: An accordion, also called a "squeeze box," makes music when the musician expands and contracts the instrument. Similarly, a presenter can use an outline to adapt to different time constraints. The key points stay the same, but you will need to eliminate less-compelling details and confine yourself to the information that is most relevant to your listener, or to add information in response to a request for more. You will need to devote more or less time to each of your points—depending on the time limits your client or management team has imposed—to still deliver a powerful and tailored talk. This kind of expansion and contraction will get easier as you become more adept and experienced at balancing your time.

MISTAKE #5: MISUSING THE ALLOTTED TIME **57**

Now that we know how much time we have, it sets us up for the next confession in Scenario 2, which introduces the outline strategy to effectively manage the allotted time.

SCENARIO 2

Presenter's Confession. *I didn't use an outline because I wanted to see where the conversation would go. It wasn't as productive as I would have liked. We jumped from one topic to another, and I couldn't convey what made my company the best choice. At best, it was an overview of what we can do. At worst, it was all over the place.*

Listener's Observation. *The speaker seemed unprepared, and their talk was all over the place. A couple of times I thought, "Where are they going with this?" We didn't get the substance we were looking for, nor did we hear anything that prompted us to take the next step.*

Solution. Use an Outline

Create an outline to manage your content and deliver a presentation that has progression and still lets you speak conversationally within the time you have been given.

Having a solid framework for your presentation or talk is critical to managing the content so that it works in concert with your timing. It may initially seem odd to include timing and structure as part of creativity, but as you explore the art of crafting your message to have bigger impact, you will see that the framework is at the core of getting creative with how your message will beautifully come to life! Think of your structure as the skeleton of your presentation. Organizing your outline is essential to controlling the length of your talk and central to creating the persuasive architecture of your message. (Delivering it with oratorial flair will take a little more time, but with practice you will be able to accomplish that, too.) With skilled organization of your arguments, a deft use of speech supports and transitions, and a clear call to action, your message will connect with your listeners.

The easiest way to break it down is to consider the components of a typical presentation. Your outline includes:

- ▶ Introduction
- ▶ Body with main three points:
  - Talking Point #1
  - Talking Point #2
  - Talking Point #3
- ▶ Conclusion
- ▶ Close

At this point, it's also important to weave Monroe's Motivated Sequence—Attention Step, Need Step, Satisfaction Step, Visualization Step, and Action Step—into your outline.

The following one-page outline is an easy go-to tool to help you quickly and effectively build the foundation for your talks and meetings moving forward.

MISTAKE #5: MISUSING THE ALLOTTED TIME **59**

Presentation Ready

PRESENTATION OUTLINE WORKSHEET

I. INTRODUCTION: **(Attention Step)**

- Grab the listener's attention: (Establish a friendly feeling and arouse audience curiosity.)
  ....

- Tell the listener where you are going:
  ....

II. BODY

1. Talking Point #1 *(Ex. Why Me?)*
   a. Argument: **(Need Step)** ....
   b. Proof and/or illustration: **(Satisfaction Step)** ....
   ....
   c. So what? What this means to you is . . . **(Visualization Step)**
   ....

2. Talking Point #2 *(Ex. Why My Organization/Company?)*
   a. Argument: **(Need Step)** ....
   b. Proof and/or illustration: **(Satisfaction Step)** ....
   ....
   c. So what? What this means to you is . . . **(Visualization Step)**
   ....

3. Talking Point #3 *(Ex. Why Now?)*
   a. Argument: **(Need Step)** ....
   b. Proof and/or illustration: **(Satisfaction Step)** ....
   ....
   c. So what? What this means to you is . . . **(Visualization Step)**
   ....

III. CONCLUSION: WRAP UP (Transition into Action Step)

- Reiterate the three points **(Conclude the Visualization Step)**
  ....

- **Optional:** Suggest a couple of intriguing topics that you can discuss with the listener in your next appointment. (Give the person a reason to want to hear more.)
  ....

IV. CLOSE: CALL TO ACTION **(Action Step)**

- Make your offer of service. State what you want to happen as a result of your presentation. (For example: "It is my goal to learn more about your needs and how I might be of service to your company...") This serves as a soft transition to your close.
  ....

- Ask for the next appointment time, referral, lead, introduction, opportunity, or whatever will help you initiate the next step in the process.
  ....

Drafting Your Presentation Outline Worksheet

Make copies and fill in the blanks in the Presentation Outline Worksheet to customize your content for each opportunity.

Let's review each section to help you build your next outline and incorporate additional material and ideas moving forward.

Writing the Introduction

What you say in the first few minutes of your talk has the potential to make your audience sit up and say, "Wow! This sounds interesting!" The introduction also acts as a road map, telling listeners where your talk is headed. As you craft a well-rounded introduction:

- ▶ **Grab their attention.** Open with a statement that everyone in your audience can understand, one with universal context and a point of common reference. Create an awakening in your listeners' minds and spark their curiosity.

- ▶ **Use signposts.** Create anchor words or phrases that serve as mental signposts to provide a road map of where you are going with your talk.

- ▶ **Transition smoothly.** Use phrases that plainly bridge the gap between two different thoughts and ideas. It can be as simple as saying, "At this point, I would like to discuss _____" or "Now that we have covered A and B, let's move on to C and D."

Writing the Body

The body of your presentation contains the bulk of your message. It should have three main points. Why three main points? Researchers Suzanne B. Shu

MISTAKE #5: MISUSING THE ALLOTTED TIME **61**

and Kurt A. Carlson explored the "charm of three," a pattern that suggests increasing the number of claims about a product or service improves consumer perceptions until the fourth claim. Once you add that fourth item, some people's eyes glaze over. As the number of your points goes up, your audience's ability to recall those points goes down.

You want your listeners to remember the most important things you tell them, and three is a manageable number. To move them toward choosing you, ask and answer these simple questions: *Why do business with you? Why do business with your company? Why do it now?* If you are not answering these three questions at the outset of your presentation, chances are you need to further develop your persuasive case.

Conclusion

After you finish supporting all three of your body points, it's time to wrap up. This is where you tell your listeners what you told them. An effective conclusion has up to five distinct sections:

1. Quick summary of the information already presented
2. Appeal for your listener to act
3. Statement of your personal intent (specific steps you will take to move the transaction forward)
4. Reference to your introduction (to bookend your talk)
5. (Optional) Powerful closing phrase to emphasize your overall point

Close

This is your specific call to action: what you want your listener to do next or what your client or prospect must do to complete the transaction. It might be signing the contract or setting the next appointment time.

SCENARIO 3

Presenter's Confession. *Looking back, I realize I should have gotten to the point faster. My talk ran too long, and the customer had to immediately log off our video call. The close was awkward and abrupt, and I don't think they're interested in a follow-up meeting.*

Listener's observation. *The speaker ran way over time despite our cues to wrap it up. It was too long, and we didn't have time at the end to ask any questions. In addition, they almost made us late for our next meeting.*

Solution. Honor and Be Respectful of the Time Parameters You Have Been Given

When prospects say they want you to speak for 30 minutes, it doesn't mean you should stretch it to 40, nor does it mean you should stop at 15.

They gave you 30, so why wouldn't you thoroughly use the time you have been given? Let's look at both missteps. When speakers fail to get to the point, their talks come across as dull and jumbled, and their listeners tune out. Conversely, some speakers rush through their talks, glossing over key points and spending too little time explaining their ideas. Consider the example of a senior editor at a large publishing firm who delivered brief overviews of the books in the company's new fall line. She summed up each book in 30 seconds, and the meeting ended an hour early. While some staffers were delighted that the meeting was over so quickly, not everyone was pleased. Because she had offered such brief descriptions, the sales force didn't have the ammunition it needed to pitch the company's new titles. The lesson? She could have used the entire time more productively by building dazzling mini reviews of each book to inspire and excite the members of the sales team.

More with Less

Legendary speaker and trainer Floyd Wickman once recounted that his mentor, Zig Ziglar, told him, "If you want to make a story or a presentation better, tell it shorter." Many speakers find it hard to understand how this strategy can be effective. The power lies in the self-editing. Think of the power of the 30-second greeting card commercial that never fails to tug at our heartstrings and connects with a wide range of audiences. Those pithy commercials have been written, rewritten, expanded, and condensed to fit within a set number of seconds.

The Overnight Presentation

What if you don't have a lot of time to prepare for a presentation? What if you must complete it in a matter of hours or days?

The secret to successful overnight preparation lies in carefully planning what to say. Start by using a blank Presentation Opportunity General Information Form (page 6) and Presentation Outline Worksheet (page 59). Review your main ideas and talking points. You may find you can simply fill in the blanks. Follow the outline, and it will see you through to a successful conclusion. The result will be a logical, formulated, and convincing presentation that is persuasive rather than just informative.

Keep these templates handy so that you can craft new outlines when preparing for new opportunities. The more often you create outlines, the easier it will be.

Sample Scenario

Let's put this all together in one sample scenario. Consider the story of Kari, a writer and editor with a 30-year track record of success working for newspapers and magazines. Most people would think this is enough to keep her steadily employed, right? Unfortunately, economic and industry

64 PRESENTATION READY

challenges have taken their toll on advertising nationwide, and newspapers, magazines, and other online media outlets are making deep cuts and scaling back on personnel hours.

Kari wants to supplement her income and have more personal control over her financial situation, so she decides to treat economic challenges like the opportunity they are and build her entrepreneurial platform to generate additional freelance work. She knows that she can earn money as a freelancer, because each day more companies are forgoing full-time employees and hiring contract workers. To fully capitalize on this sea change and sell herself into new opportunities, Kari needs a winning presentation she can deliver to potential clients, who may or may not know that they need her.

Her first step is to use the Presentation Opportunity General Information Form (page 6). She answered the simple questions (as shown in the completed form on page 65). With this information in hand, Kari put together a brief presentation using the Drafting Your Persuasive Presentation (Long Outline) worksheet (see pages 66–68). Use this sample as a guideline whenever you need to deliver a general talk. You will see that this specific example can be delivered in a more conversational manner in a one-on-one setting if you focus on the talking points rather than on the actual words of the text.

Now review the Short Outline Form sample that follows on page 69. Notice how we condensed the core outline and key points and phrases and transferred them to an index card to use in the field. You'll still verbally communicate all the material from your long outline. The short version just serves as a "cheat sheet" to help you recall your six main components while you are presenting.

MISTAKE #5: MISUSING THE ALLOTTED TIME **65**

> *Presentation* Ready

SAMPLE
PRESENTATION OPPORTUNITY
GENERAL INFORMATION FORM

I. WHAT IS THE GOAL (OR INTENTION) OF YOUR PRESENTATION?
To craft a general elevator speech that I can use at a business networking breakfast in two days. I hope to introduce who I am and how I can be of service and to set up one-on-one appointment times with potential clients.

II. AUDIENCE ANALYSIS INFORMATION

- Who are the listeners? *Small to midsize businesses*

- Audience size? *Approximately 50 attendees*

- Average age of group? *21 to 60*

- Gender ratio? *Mixed/unknown*

- Attitude of audience? *Busy, come together to network, share ideas*

- How informed is the audience? *No idea, I am new.*

III. LOGISTICAL INFORMATION

- In person, virtual, or hybrid *In person - meeting room at a local hotel*

- Visual aid options *None (I guess I could hold up a sample of my work)*

- Time allotted for presentation *3 minutes*

- Who speaks before/after you *Two other new members*

IV. WHAT IS THE BEST WAY TO CLOSE IN THIS SITUATION?
They are in hurry, and I have to sit down right after I speak, so I will pass out my card and give them a simple handout, "The Top 10 Reasons to Write a White Paper in Today's Market." I will invite them to come see me after the meeting if they would like to set up an appointment time, and I will follow up with them later.

SAMPLE

PRESENTATION OUTLINE WORKSHEET (LONG VERSION)

I. INTRODUCTION: **(Attention Step)**
- Grab the listener's attention:

    Good morning . . . Imagine yourself in the following scenario. You have been tasked with writing an article for your company newsletter. After hours of frustrating attempts, your computer screen and notepad are still blank. You're not feeling creative. The deadline is approaching. Your writer's block is costing you time and money. What are you going to do? Maybe this scenario isn't so imaginary. If this example is your reality now or possibly in the future, you don't have to go it alone. My name is Kari B. and I might be the solution to your challenge.

- Tell the listener where you are going:

    You might not know that people like me exist. I am a freelance writer with the ability to pen everything from memos and white papers to marketing materials and feature profiles. During the next few minutes, I'd like to tell you how I can give you peace of mind, save you time, and save you money by using my skills to be your professional writer.

II. BODY
1. Talking Point #1 *(Ex. Why Me?)*
    a. Argument: **(Need Step)**

    I can provide you with peace of mind in challenging situations. (Need Step) Have you ever had one of those moments when you knew exactly what you wanted to say but couldn't find the words? (Satisfaction Step) That's where I come in. I have the skills to listen and put your ideas into written form. (Visualization Step) When you partner with me, you will get accurate and authentic messaging as if you had written it yourself.

MISTAKE #5: MISUSING THE ALLOTTED TIME **67**

Presentation Ready

b. Proof and/or illustration: **(Satisfaction Step)**

I am an experienced professional with a degree in journalism. I have specialized in writing and editing.

c. So what? What this means to you is . . . **(Visualization Step)**

What this means to you is, again, peace of mind. No longer will you have to stress out over getting your point across or a looming deadline for a written project. My job is to make you look good.

2. Talking Point #2 *(Ex. Why My Organization/Company?)*
   a. Argument: **(Need Step)**

   I can save you time. As I work on a contract basis, you will be able to funnel assignments to me on your schedule and at your convenience, freeing you up to concentrate on other tasks.

   b. Proof and/or illustration: **(Satisfaction Step)**

   How do I do this? I have 18 years of experience in newsrooms where I learned to write fast and accurately. My freelance clients often depend on me to produce materials in as little as 48 to 72 hours.

   c. So what? What this means to you is . . . **(Visualization Step)**

   What this means to you is that instead of investing hours in a written project, you can set aside just a few minutes to share your thoughts with me, and then I will have the information I need to proceed, leaving you to move on to other important matters.

3. Talking Point #3 *(Ex. Why Now?)*
   a. Argument: **(Need Step)**

   In today's challenging economy, I can save you money by working as an independent contractor.

(continued on next page)

68 PRESENTATION READY

Presentation Ready

b. Proof and/or illustration: **(Satisfaction Step)**

My business model is designed to fill in the missing puzzle piece in your company. I offer a competitive rate and have saved many organizations the headache of hiring and training an in-house staff writer.

c. So what? What this means to you is ... **(Visualization Step)**

What this means to you is . . . I can save you the investment of a full-time employee, and give you the opportunity to use that money elsewhere in your business.

III. CONCLUSION: WRAP UP (Transition into Action Step)

- Reiterate the three points **(Conclude the Visualization Step)**

So, the next time you are faced with a deadline, or before you get writer's block, I hope you'll pick up the phone and call me first. You don't have to "go it alone." Maybe I can help you with that newsletter article. I can offer you peace of mind, save you time, and maybe even save you some money.

IV. CLOSE: CALL TO ACTION **(Action Step)**

- Make your offer of service. State what you want to happen as a result of your presentation.

It's my goal to be the writer you choose to work with on your projects.

- Ask for the next appointment time, referral, lead, introduction, opportunity, or whatever will help you initiate the next step in the process.

Please come see me after the meeting today and let's set up an appointment to discuss your needs and how I might be of service. When we get together, I will also give you this complimentary tip sheet on the "Top 10 Reasons to Write a White Paper in Today's Market." Thank you for sharing your time with me today.

Presentation Ready

SHORT OUTLINE FORM (4X6 CARD)

SAMPLE

I. INTRODUCTION

• **Grab the listener's attention:** Scenario. *Your writer's block is costing you time and money. What are you going to do?*

• **Tell them where you are going:** I am a freelance writer with the ability to pen everything from memos and white papers to marketing materials and feature profiles. *Today, I want to briefly share with you how I can...*

II. BODY

• **Talking Point #1: Why Me? Argument:** *Give you "peace of mind" in challenging situations. When you partner with me, you will get accurate and authentic messaging as if you had written it yourself*

• **Talking Point #2: Why My Organization/Company? Argument:** *Save you time. As I work on a contract basis, you will be able to funnel assignments to me on your schedule and at your convenience freeing you up to concentrate on other tasks*

• **Talking point #3:** *In today's challenging economy, I can save you money by working as an independent contractor*

III. CONCLUSION

• **Wrap up –Reiterate the three points:** *You don't have to "go it alone." Maybe I can help you with that newsletter article. I can offer you peace of mind, save you time, and maybe even save you some money.*

IV. CLOSE: CALL TO ACTION

Ask for Next Appointment: *Offer the complimentary tip sheet on the "Top 10 Reasons to Write a White Paper in Today's Market"*

70 PRESENTATION READY

Note: Every presentation is different. Your main talking points might be different from the points we used here.

Making this type of outline in advance of your presentation is essential. The benefits include:

- ▶ Helps map the course of your message so you know where to put evidence, stories, and illustrations. These contribute to making clear and memorable points. (We will discuss these more in the next chapter, which addresses the mistake of being boring, boring, boring.)

- ▶ Provides clarity and control of the information when navigating time-related issues.

- ▶ Keeps the speaker from straying off course.

- ▶ Creates a clear, logical format, which helps the audience retain more information.

Summary

Mistake #5 is misusing the allotted time, resulting in a critical imbalance of content. This could include running out of time to make key points, spending too little time on key points, or simply lacking awareness of the time you've been given.

- Building a balanced presentation within specific time parameters is a key part of becoming an effective presenter.
- Think of your structure as the skeleton of your presentation. Remember the accordion. When you speak from an outline, you can expand and contract any of your key points to ensure that your talk works well within the time allotted.
- The one-page outline is a go-to tool to help you quickly and effectively build a foundation for your talk.
- A typical presentation has six components: introduction, three body points, conclusion, and close. Pair this typical structure with Monroe's Motivated Sequence to begin crafting the outline for your next talk.
- To balance your presentation's content with the time available to present it, divide the number of components in your presentation by the amount of time you have to deliver your message. For example, a 30-minute presentation divided by 6 components equals approximately 5 minutes per component.
- The overnight or last-minute presentation is not impossible. Start with the blank Presentation Opportunity General Information Form, then work through the easy-to-use Presentation Outline Worksheet (extemporaneous format). These tools will help you get started.

▶ **Next Up.** Mistake #6: Being Boring, Boring, Boring

MISTAKE #6

Being Boring, Boring, Boring

DEFINITION
Giving a presentation that is dull, tedious, or tiresome; failing to generate interest, curiosity, or intrigue, and causing your audience to become restless or weary.

In the previous chapter, we outlined the basic structure of a persuasive message and established the importance of crafting a balanced presentation. Now we will explore how to incorporate the entertainment factor of creativity into your next talk.

Understanding the Issue of Being Boring, Boring, Boring

Boring presentations are unfortunately a common occurrence. Multiple factors can contribute to a dull, tedious, and tiresome talk, including low presenter energy, an overall lack of creativity, and an absence of storytelling and other entertaining elements.

The State of Sales Presentations research study found that being boring was the number one mistake the participants saw others commit during their presentations, but it was not initially a mistake participants identified in themselves. "I'm informative," they said. "Other people are boring."

It is a tricky topic. Presenters don't ever want to be seen as boring, and it's not something people typically want to tell a colleague or friend. "Sorry, but you're not a very engaging speaker. Your talk was kind of boring."

The problem with boring presentations may seem obvious; yet people continue to give them again and again. Many business professionals don't realize how truly uninteresting their presentations are unless they are able to watch themselves in a video playback situation. Then they will often say, "Maybe I did ramble a bit," or "Maybe it was a little bit boring."

When asked why they kept going, some admit to simply wanting to get through the material. Others tend to blame the nature of what they're selling: "It's not my fault I'm boring. I have to share a lot of facts and figures and get through a great deal of content." But what is the point of presenting the information if nobody's really listening to what you're saying? Still others blame their audience for being tuned out and lifeless, but the burden does not lie with the listener. It always lies with the presenter.

Think of a presentation that surprised you in the best possible way. You sat down expecting to hear only what you had heard before, but a few minutes into the talk, the speaker had you intrigued. You couldn't entirely pinpoint whether it was the speaker's use of humor, charming stories, or engaging questions, but it jolted you awake and had you listening with an open mind. That's the goal with this chapter.

As you will see, the issue of being boring often overlaps with other mistakes addressed in the next two chapters of this book. For the purposes of this chapter, we will focus on two specific issues.

A Few Real-World Confessions

Our study results showed that salespeople who made boring presentations failed to (1) use speech supports and storytelling to inspire thought, analysis, and understanding of the message and (2) put themselves in the seat of the listener to determine whether the message was entertaining and enjoyable.

As with any mistake, to avoid making it, you need to understand how it manifests in the real world. Let's explore what some of our research participants said about being boring, boring, boring.

SCENARIO 1

Presenter's Confession. *I'm not a storyteller. I'm a facts and numbers guy. I don't need to tell a story because the data speaks for itself, and I have been doing this for 30 years.*

Listener's Observation. *The presenter was clearly knowledgeable, but quite frankly, their talk was boring. There were lots of facts and figures but no personal touch, customization, or illustrations. It was flat, like they were on autopilot.*

Solution. Use Speech Supports and Storytelling to Inspire Thought and Understanding of the Message

> If you would persuade, you must appeal
> to interest rather than intellect.
> —BENJAMIN FRANKLIN

Many seasoned professionals have been giving the same presentation for so long, they can unconsciously slip into autopilot. They throw out too many facts and rely on the same old stories. But in today's competitive market, it might be time to hit the refresh button on your material. Yesterday's go-to presentation is not necessarily going to capture or maintain the attention of today's prospects. It's a waste of time and creates a dated image of you and your company. If you can't keep your listeners' attention, you won't connect with them. No connection means there's no communication and nothing is going to happen at the end of your meeting.

Your best strategy is to step into the challenge of getting creative, whether you are presenting in person or via a video platform. Your creativity goal should focus on two things:

- ▶ Crafting a message that is memorable, influential, and intriguing
- ▶ Being entertaining and engaging—maybe even making your audience laugh—and getting them thinking

76 PRESENTATION READY

The key to doing this is to remember that the presentation is about *the listeners*; it's not just about you or your company. If you want it to land, it needs to consistently circle back to them and how it can help or serve them. In Chapter 5, we likened the outline structure to the skeleton. Here we create the soul of your presentation.

Speech Supports

Some of the most effective tools at your disposal are speech supports. They are the antidote for boring and can help you liven up your content and bring your message to life. Speech supports help you link your arguments and data to examples and illustrations that make your points easy to understand and relatable to the listener. They have the power to boost your credibility while drawing in your prospect's attention.

One of the most effective speech supports is the anecdote or story, usually showing up as a short, engaging tale that makes your point in an entertaining way. When time is a factor, you don't always have the luxury of sharing a lengthy story, but there are tools to help you bring a little flair to your presentation.

Other popular and useful speech supports include:

- **Analogy.** A similarity between the features of two things, on which a comparison may be based. "A good public relations department is to a sports team franchise as fuel is to a jet."

- **Definition.** The formal statement of the meaning or significance of a word or phrase. "A speech, as defined by *Webster's*, is the practice of oral communication."

The rhetorical device, which helps speakers evoke an emotional response, is also an effective speech support. Rhetorical devices include:

MISTAKE #6: BEING BORING, BORING, BORING **77**

- **Alliteration.** The repetition of the sound of a particular letter within a sentence. "A bright, bilingual broker is just what your company needs to boost its bottom line!"

- **Anaphora.** Emphasizing words by repeating them at the beginning of neighboring clauses. This was a device used by then-Senator Barack Obama with great success during his 2008 presidential campaign. Here is an example from his January 2008 New Hampshire Primary speech:

> **We will** harness the ingenuity of farmers and scientists, citizens, and entrepreneurs to free this nation from the tyranny of oil and save our planet from a point of no return. And when I am president of the United States, **we will** end this war in Iraq and bring our troops home. . . . **We will** end this war in Iraq. **We will** bring our troops home. **We will** finish the job—**we will** finish the job against Al Qaida in Afghanistan. **We will** care for our veterans. **We will** restore our moral standing in the world.

His use of anaphora helped engage the audience and encouraged people to join in, some repeating each phrase at just the appropriate time in cadence with the speaker. As the message progressed, Obama created a sense of unity between himself and the audience.

- **Antithesis.** The use of contrasting words or phrases. Legendary astronaut Neil Armstrong used this device during the 1969 moon landing: "That's one small step for man. One giant leap for mankind."

- **Personification.** Giving human qualities to an inanimate object. "Lightning danced across the sky. The wind howled in the night."

- **Rhetorical question.** A question to which an answer is not expected. "How many of you have ever had a bad day?"

78 PRESENTATION READY

▶ **Aposiopesis.** The act of leaving a thought incomplete, usually by suddenly breaking off in speech, as in "Why, you little—!" The speaker leaves a sentence unfinished so the listeners can finish it for themselves.

▶ **Metaphor.** Equating two things in a way that emphasizes their similarity. Everyday conversations and writing are full of metaphors: "Laughter is the best medicine."

While it would be nice to have the wit and charm of a professional comedian and always be ready with the perfect quip, that's not realistic. If you want a creative, engaging presentation, you will have to work for it. That means starting with a bit of fresh research. Start by collecting stories, magazine articles, and funny or compelling one-liners. Save them for ongoing use, and keep a lookout for additional material that really hits home for you. Mine your own life and personal experiences. Some of the best material comes from our personal, academic, and professional lives. Remember, there is validity to sayings such as, "You can't make this stuff up!" and "Truth is stranger than fiction!" If you are feeling stuck, consider sharing a real-world personal story of how you and your product saved the day for a similar client or customer in the past.

A Little Creative Spin

Now that you have your tools in hand, it's time to put the puzzle together. Review your outline, arguments, and evidence, and then begin to pair some of your creative illustrations and speech supports with your most salient talking points. This is going to take a little finessing, but when you find the perfect anecdote to pair with timely evidence, you can make your data and arguments come to life. Touching back to the image of the scales in Chapter 3, remember to balance your storytelling and speech supports with case evidence.

The more fun you have with your presentations, the more fun your audience will have listening to them.

Consider the efforts of sales professional Tom Bayer, who worked for a major mortgage banking company. He would start his presentations by saying, "Hi, I'm Tom Bayer, as in Bayer Aspirin. I am not related to that Bayer family, but I am the lender who can take the headache out of the lending process for you." He then would gracefully transition into the body of his talk, explaining how he could eliminate various "headaches" that might come up during a lending transaction. Bayer's approach was light, funny, and not too cheesy. Best of all, it was memorable.

A Bit of Pushback
I'm Stuck. I Have No Idea How to Get More Creative.

Here are a few ideas to help you trigger a more creative mindset and stimulate some fresh concepts:

- ▶ Read things that you don't ordinarily read in the course of your daily life.
- ▶ Listen to podcasts and audiobooks.
- ▶ Attend courses, webinars, and conferences.
- ▶ Read journals, magazines, and newspapers.
- ▶ Create brainstorming groups and join in co-creating opportunities.
- ▶ Find a role model or get a mentor.
- ▶ Watch television and movies and go to comedy shows to stay abreast of pop culture.
- ▶ Evaluate other speakers and presenters.
- ▶ Conduct interviews with customers and competitors.

80 PRESENTATION READY

This notion of using speech supports doesn't mean you have to be an entertainer. It's about putting thoughtful consideration into crafting messages that inspire curiosity, create awakenings, and give your listener something to contemplate.

SCENARIO 2

Presenter's Confession. *I don't think I'm a very good presenter. I'm not Meryl Streep!*

Listener's Observation. *The presenter didn't have much energy or show any passion about their product. They didn't seem to be having fun—and we certainly weren't—which made their talk feel twice as long.*

Solution. Put Yourself in the Shoes of a Skeptical Listener to Determine Whether the Message Is Intriguing and Thought-Provoking

It might seem simple and obvious, but as you practice your presentation, ask yourself if your audience will find it interesting. If you hear that small voice saying, "I think this is boring," then it probably is. If you want your audience to stay alert and focused, your message must be lively enough to hold their attention. How often have you had the experience of speaking with someone who didn't particularly want you there? Part of the responsibility of a sales professional is to meet with people who initially didn't want them there. The task is to pique your listeners' curiosity, turn them around, and make them pleased that they shared their time with you.

> Somebody is boring me. I think it's me.
>
> —DYLAN THOMAS

Meeting this kind of challenge is beautifully demonstrated in the 1996 film *The Mirror Has Two Faces*, which stars Barbra Streisand as Rose and Jeff Bridges as Gregory. It is a rich and clever tale about two people who

MISTAKE #6: BEING BORING, BORING, BORING **81**

agree to an unconventional relationship, get married, and ultimately fall in love.

Both Rose and Gregory teach at Columbia University. She's a professor of literature, and he's a professor of calculus. The two have never met, and they are about to be set up on a date. Gregory wants to see what Rose is like before they go out, so he pops into one of her lectures. He sits down in the class with hundreds of students and sees Rose leading the class in an engaging presentation with lots of juicy material and fantastic style. She clearly has an incredible connection with the audience. They love her! She is real and raw and speaking beautifully in her own voice. Rose checks up on Gregory, too. As he teaches calculus, some of his students fall asleep while others try to sneak out.

During their first date, Gregory mentions to Rose that he dropped by her class, compliments her teaching style, and asks, "How do you get them to stay?"

"You need to relate to your students," Rose tells Gregory. "Your back is to the class, and it seems as if you are having a math party and you only invited yourself." She says that he needs to relax and have fun, tell a story, maybe put some humor into it.

Gregory and Rose continue to date, and eventually they are married. Rose is a baseball fan, and one day while watching a game, Gregory says, "I've never understood the fascination with baseball."

"Really?" Rose says. "Actually, the game should really interest you, as it is all about statistics and averages." She then proceeds to explain the game from a mathematical perspective.

Flash forward to Gregory's next day in class, where the scene is typical. He's droning on, students are slipping into comas, and then he stops and says, "Anybody see the game yesterday? Let me see if I can put this another way . . ." He uses the personal story about watching baseball with his wife to explain how hitting a home run relates to measuring trajectory and velocity. Suddenly his audience is awake. He's facing them. His style is coming to life, and his students are engaged in his lecture. Gregory is thrilled!

When he gets home, he tells Rose what happened and says, "I could not believe it. Suddenly the room was filled with tangible energy. . . . We were connected . . . and they stayed! I was a better teacher today than I have ever been before, because of you."

In conclusion, most of us can't see ourselves as others do. But when we try, our presentations are the better for it.

Summary

Mistake #6 is being boring, boring, boring: giving a presentation that is dull, tedious, or tiresome; failing to generate interest, curiosity, or intrigue; and causing your audience to become restless or weary.

- It's the presenter's responsibility to build and deliver an interesting message. You might think your data is interesting, but that doesn't mean the audience will.

- Speech supports such as analogies, anecdotes, and rhetorical devices are the antidotes to boring, helping speakers link their arguments to illustrations that inspire thought and make their points easy to understand.

- When you pair the perfect speech support with timely evidence, you make your data and arguments come to life. The more fun you have with your presentations, the more fun your audience will have listening to them.

- Put yourself in the seat of a skeptical listener and ask whether your message is intriguing and thought-provoking. If a small, persistent voice tells you that it's boring, it probably is!

- Even a mathematics equation can be paired with a clever illustration to awaken an audience and bring your message to life. It just takes a little effort. There is no boring material, only boring presentations.

▶ **Next Up.** Mistake #7: Ineffectively Using Visual Aids

MISTAKE #7

Ineffectively Using Visual Aids

DEFINITION
A visual aid is any sort of prop used to support a speech or presentation, including charts, graphs, slides, photographs, videos, handouts, and demonstration models. Ineffectively using a visual aid in a presentation includes a range of issues from totally lacking any to being overly dependent on them, or even using poorly crafted visual aids.

A picture is worth a thousand words.

—UNKNOWN

Understanding the Issue of Ineffectively Using Visual Aids

If charts, graphs, slides, photographs, or other props could sell a product or service on their own, organizations would not need human beings to deliver their message to listeners. As the presenter, it can be helpful to think of yourself as a symphony conductor and your visual aids as the instruments under your direction. Each instrument is unique, and it is your job to determine just the right timing and placement to create a beautiful and synchronized performance. Conductors must know how and when to amplify certain instruments at specific moments to convey exactly what the composer of the music wants the audience to experience. Speakers must do the same. Without this understanding, it's easy to ineffectively use visual aids.

As a rule, your listeners are best served when visual aids are employed to enhance—not overshadow—your message. They supplement your presentation, providing support to the body of your talk, and go beyond basic explanations to enrich the context. They are, by their very nature, intended to stimulate and engage listener attention. Visual aids can have a significant, positive impact on your presentation when you deploy them strategically, and listeners most definitely notice their use.

Advantages of incorporating visual aids into your message include:

▶ Presenters cover the same material in less time.

▶ Listeners learn and retain more.

▶ Audiences typically see presenters as more professional, persuasive, credible, interesting, and better prepared.

Presentation support materials are growing more innovative and sophisticated. Increasingly the term "visual aid" can include any sort of sensory aid—sight, sound, touch, taste, and smell—that helps an idea land with an audience. A presentation with well-placed sensory enhancements is more effective than a presentation without them.

The State of Sales Presentations research study found that many participants observed the mistake of ineffectively using visual aids in other presenters, but didn't often admit to doing it themselves.

A Few Real-World Confessions

The results from our study participants showed that sales professionals who committed the mistake of ineffectively using visual aids failed to:

1. Level up the presentation with thoughtful, stimulating aids that engage the senses

2. Remember that the visual aid is for the benefit of listeners, not a crutch to help presenters get through their own content
3. Strategically employ visual aids to supplement a presentation while maintaining engagement with listeners

To avoid making any mistake, we must understand how it manifests in the real world. Let's explore what some of our research participants said about ineffectively using visual aids.

SCENARIO 1

Presenter's Confession. *I didn't use any slides, photographs, or demonstrations in my presentation. I just wanted to sit down and have a conversation, but I think it ended up lacking the wow factor.*

Listener's Observation. *I appreciated the speaker's interest in learning more about what we needed, but we wanted to see what they could really do. It would have been nice to experience the product (service, etc.) and have a bit more of a demonstration along with the conversation.*

Solution. Level up the Presentation with Thoughtful and Stimulating Visual Appeal to Provide an Interactive Experience That Engages the Senses

If you are wondering whether using visual aids makes a difference, the answer is yes. According to a Wharton School of Business study, 67 percent of audience members were convinced by a verbal presentation that used visual support, compared with just 50 percent by a verbal-only presentation.

Some presenters overcorrect when they attempt to avoid filling their talk with too many slides and end up leaving out visual aids altogether. The trick is to find a balance between verbal and visual components (or any

88 PRESENTATION READY

component that engages the senses). Think about the compelling pitches on ABC's hit show *Shark Tank* (or BBC One's *Dragons' Den* in the United Kingdom). They allow the sharks and dragons to experience the product—taste the energy drink, lift the weights, or try on the socks. For a listener or potential customer, nothing compares to a sensory experience.

How Do You Determine When and Where to Employ Visual Aids?

Consider how you will use visual aids in the earliest stages of crafting your persuasive presentation. After finalizing your outline, ask these key questions:

- ▸ *Where can I employ a couple of great visual aids to help clarify a concept?* Focus on the ideas that you want your audience to remember when the presentation is over.

- ▸ *Does this visual aid add value and enhance the presentation? Or is it just a text-based visual, such as words or bullet points?* If you can choose, pick visual aids that vibrantly illustrate your points, sparking curiosity and discussion.

Visual Aids at Your Disposal

As you determine which visual aids to use in a presentation, you must decide whether you want to adopt a high-tech or a low-tech approach. Both kinds can easily be used properly and improperly. High-tech visual aids are nothing more than low-tech aids taken to a new level. The benefits of low-tech visual aids are that they are easy to use, while the downside is that they often lack the *wow* factor. The benefits of high-tech visual aids are that they are heavy on the *wow* factor, but on the downside they can hijack a presentation, take too long to demonstrate, and pose the risk of a tech

MISTAKE #7: INEFFECTIVELY USING VISUAL AIDS **89**

failure. As with any visual aid—whether it be a paper handout or a sophisticated piece of equipment—remember that it's an important part of the big show. You need it to work when you call on it.

Low-tech visual aids include:

- Paper handouts (fliers, cheat sheets, meeting agendas, outlines, and other collateral material)
- Samples (tasting cookies, smelling fragrances, feeling the texture of a fabric)
- Flipcharts and storyboarding (individual boards with sequenced graphs or pictures)
- Traditional whiteboards and dry-erase markers
- Working demonstrations and models (any kind of equipment from a stain remover to handicrafts or architectural models)

High-tech visual aids include:

- Elaborate slide shows and presentation decks for in person, virtual, and hybrid presentation platforms (Zoom, Microsoft Teams, WebEx, or whatever future platforms might be)
- Immersive experiences (augmented reality and virtual reality experiences)
- Video monitors with touch screens and other interactive elements
- Highlight reels and/or video clips of a product or service in use
- Live presentations with active demonstrations that inspire utility
- Holograms and holodecks

SCENARIO 2

Presenter's Confession. *I didn't want to forget the key points I wanted to make in the presentation, so I created a bullet point list. Looking back, I confess I ended up just reading off my screen instead of having a conversation with the listener. I could have been a bit more creative with my visual aid strategy.*

Listener's Observation. *Seriously? I can't believe they just read their slide deck to me. Way too much text and too many bullet points with no visuals.*

Solution. Use Significantly Fewer Bullet Point Slides and Add More Visually Stimulating Elements

The illustration above might seem quite basic, and yet tragically, it happens in business environments every day. Why? Either the presenters just didn't think about it, or they said they didn't have time to create the visual aids—but at what cost? For persuasive presenters, the idea is that seeing something is better for understanding or learning than having it described. Remember that visual aids are for the benefit of listeners, not a crutch to help presenters get through their own content.

Let's say you are a travel agent promoting a special vacation package to Bora Bora. You could make a bullet point list of the amazing qualities of this tropical paradise:

- ▶ Beautiful ocean, sandy beaches, and palm trees
- ▶ Luxury hotels and spa facilities
- ▶ Snorkeling and diving trips

MISTAKE #7: **INEFFECTIVELY USING VISUAL AIDS**   91

Before

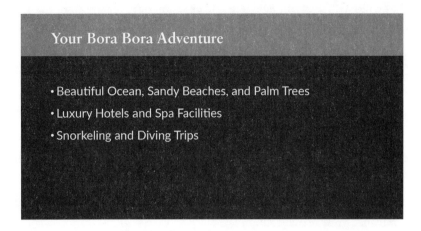

This "before" slide could be considered a visual aid, but it's just text—not a picture. A more compelling visual aid would be a photo or video clip of people playing in beautiful ocean waters, walking in the morning on the white sandy beaches, resting under swaying palm trees, dining at luxury hotels, and viewing sea life on snorkeling and diving trips. Those are true visual aids that land with an audience much more effectively than a bullet point slide.

After

It's been said that a picture is worth a thousand words, but what does it say? The most effective images activate emotion or reveal more of the argument, narrative, or idea that a speaker is imparting to an audience. Pictures expand and move the conversation forward, and that's why they must be chosen carefully and placed strategically so that they amplify your message.

With technology dramatically changing the presentation landscape, speakers have countless choices when it comes to visual enhancements that illustrate their ideas. In that abundance, some presenters can lose sight of their own responsibility. They relinquish their power to high-tech tools, expecting these slick devices to do the selling for them. Explore options that could work in any given situation—just be sure to select visual aids that advance your presentation.

Here are some helpful guidelines to remember when incorporating visual aids:

- ▶ Make sure each visual aid has a clear purpose. Does it illustrate or say something visually that you can't convey in the same way verbally?

- ▶ Less is more: Don't use too many. If you do, they might lose their impact and bore your audience.

- ▶ Keep it simple and easy to understand. If your aids include numbers and words, make them large and easy to read.

- ▶ Design, branding, and color can enhance visual aids, making them pleasing to the eye and helping to emphasize your points. Use them to spice up an otherwise flat and boring graph, but don't overdo it. Professional-grade polish or homespun? It simply depends on your style.

- ▶ Think about the *wow* factor. That is, does it make people say, "wow!" and get excited?

- ▶ When you use text, emphasize no more than three items. (Remember the charm of three, discussed in Chapter 5.)

MISTAKE #7: INEFFECTIVELY USING VISUAL AIDS 93

Ultimately, both high- and low-tech presentation supports can be incredibly helpful, but there is still no substitute for the human touch. The visual aids at your disposal are subordinate to you. If they upstage you, you may lose control of your presentation. More about that in Scenario 3.

Creatively Blending Text and Images

Here's a fun example of someone using carefully curated images in a creative way to assure potential clients that she understood their specific needs. In the middle of the coronavirus pandemic, a woman named Kari (pronounced like *Ferr"ari"*) Gillenwater was working with a financial services company to deliver internal organization presentations. Like many people at the time, the company owners were stressed about a wide range of challenges, and she was planning to address these pain points in her talk. These challenges included advisors who felt like the pandemic was holding them back and others who suddenly found themselves working remotely and juggling constant interruptions from kids, pets, and spouses. To ensure that her message landed with just the right tone—classy but with a little wry humor—she decided to go beyond the usual, boring bullet point slide listing the company's challenges. Keeping in mind that the company's brand mascot is a regal lion, she jumped onto Pinterest, and in about 30 minutes, found a collection of lion photos that perfectly illustrated many of the stressors the company's workforce was experiencing.

The beautiful outdoor shots—of lions looking exhausted, weighed down with cubs, and wrestling with other lions—were an instant hit with her audience. They not only heard the challenges that employees were dealing with; they also *saw* them. The photos she chose were relevant and relatable but also witty and fun, and they helped soften a stressful time while also driving home her main points (see image on the next page).

This is a simple pivot that doesn't require weeks of work or research. When prepping for your next presentation, look at your bullet points or other key pieces of text and find photos or video clips to say the same thing. Remember, sometimes doing little things can make a big difference.

SCENARIO 3

Presenter's Confession. *Our team put together some great slides and pictures, but on the video call, the pictures were the only thing the audience saw. Each slide was up too long. We should have done a better job of toggling back and forth between our faces with virtual eye contact and the slides to create a connection.*

Listener's Observation. *It would have been better if they had just cut down the number of slides and used two or three to make the point. It felt like we were in a webinar rather than a business presentation, and we needed more engagement with the speaker.*

Solution. Strategically Employ Visual Aids to Supplement Your Presentation While Staying Engaged with Listeners

Consider this effort from Dan Bliven, a business development professional at a manufacturing firm. Before the coronavirus pandemic, Bliven spent

MISTAKE #7: INEFFECTIVELY USING VISUAL AIDS

most of his time out in the field and on the road, demonstrating a range of products at trade shows. When the pandemic lockdown started, those trade shows ended. On the remote video calls that replaced them, Bliven showed slides and talked about what he used to do. That's what most people were doing at the time. But he was frustrated that he couldn't physically be in front of his customers, and he feared his listeners were bored with his slide presentation.

Eager to level up, Bliven asked himself what he could do to generate a little more buzz:

> I found that the adage "Where there's a will, there's a way" definitely applied. With the support of my manager, Matt Gravette, we brainstormed how we could be different and connect with our customers, which led to the creation of the home-based studio! What that really means is I dusted off my old trade show booth and set it up in my garage. The effort evolved over time to include lighting, technology, and props. We held rehearsals, and it worked!

Soon Bliven was receiving compliments from customers for making such a creative effort, and eventually his peers began developing their own home studios.

This story is just one example of the many pivots you can use to take your presentations to the next level. With a little creativity and an emphasis on what is possible—instead of dwelling on what is impossible—the results can be revolutionary.

A Bit of Pushback
What if My Laptop Crashes or Equipment Malfunctions? What Can I Do if a Quick Fix isn't Possible?

These are great questions that we will dive into when we discuss Mistake #11: Technology or Demonstration Failures. The short answer is to have a low-tech backup plan and be prepared to use it. Practice your talk using your visual aids. Get comfortable with the technology. Shift from your high-tech aids to low-tech alternatives as you practice your presentation, ensuring that you can do it comfortably. This way you will head off possible problems before they arise. Evaluate your performance, and make sure your visuals enhance rather than detract from your presentation.

"I need someone well versed in the art of torture—do you know PowerPoint?"
Source: Reprinted with permission from Cartoonstock.com.

In conclusion, tragically, the classic phrase "death by PowerPoint," as referenced in the cartoon above, still applies. Why? Because overuse of slide decks is a persistent problem. Presenters are still struggling with how to best use their visual aids, and it's an area that you can improve on for better results.

Summary

Mistake #7 is ineffectively using visual aids: includes a range of issues from totally lacking any to being overly dependent on them, or even using poorly crafted visual aids.

- Visual aids energize your listeners and help them understand your points faster.

- Visual aids are for the benefit of listeners, not a crutch to help presenters get through their own content.

- A visual aid is intended to show something visually that you can't verbally express in the same way.

- Review the six basic rules governing the use of visual aids.

- Don't rely on your visual aids to do all the work. Place them strategically, and tie them to a specific purpose within your presentation.

▶ **Next Up.** Mistake #8: Failure to Create Connection with Listeners

MISTAKE #8

Failure to Create Connection with Listeners

DEFINITION
The inability to establish a genuine and authentic personal and professional bond with an audience or decision maker. Failing to read the room, understand the prevailing mood, and adjust your presentation accordingly.

Understanding the Issue of Failing to Create Connection with Listeners

When examining an individual's overall message, it can be difficult to pinpoint why certain presenters connect with some audiences and not others. People generally tend to gravitate toward those with whom they share interests, outlooks, and values. Speakers and listeners might also bond over mutual challenges, concerns, and dislikes. There are many different levels and kinds of connection, and establishing a rapport with an audience exists on an ever-changing continuum.

Entrepreneur Patrick Henry is very intentional about the people he does business with, and he's always on the lookout for genuine partners and reliable connections. To that end, he selects team members, clients, and other partners based on how well they pass what he calls "the boat test." After weighing what he knows and has observed firsthand, he asks himself if he'd want to spend four to six hours on a boat with that person. Would the person be fun, safe, interesting, and dependable and have any of the other qualities needed for a pleasant day on the water? The answer determines whether he moves the relationship forward.

This chapter explores the dynamic, nuanced subject of connection and its significant effect on persuasive communication. Connection drives action. History and data have repeatedly demonstrated that speakers who form a connection with their listeners are more likely to persuade them to listen, change their minds, or decide to act. It makes sense, and yet it remains a sticking point for today's professionals.

The process of building connection can seem a bit mysterious and subjective, but we can quantify parts of it by analyzing what it means to fall short in this area. In the State of Sales Presentations research study, participants provided examples of observed behaviors relating to the mistake of failing to create connection with listeners, which include:

- ▶ Not listening to clients
- ▶ Failing to understand and adapt to audience concerns
- ▶ Interrupting the audience
- ▶ Doing a poor job of acknowledging audience cues
- ▶ Doing most of the talking and not engaging with the audience
- ▶ Not pausing to determine if the information is of value to the listener
- ▶ Stereotyping or prejudging prospects
- ▶ Not asking enough questions to create engagement
- ▶ Speaking in an unfriendly or off-putting style

Ouch! While no one does these things intentionally, they happen every day. Most speakers intuitively know the importance of connecting with listeners, but the above missteps are all too common. One reason speakers fail to create connection is that they spend more time on explaining their product or service and too little time on setting the mood and establishing the common ground that will help bridge the gap between them and their listeners.

What can persuasive speakers do to hone their ability to create connection? The answer to this question includes exploring a speaker's personal communication style as well as the substance of the message being shared. We will delve into style in the next section on delivery. In this chapter, we will explore substance.

Aristotle's fourth-century work *Rhetoric* contains a classic, even timeless, formula that can be applied to any persuasive presentation to build a better, stronger connection with listeners. Aristotle believed that establishing a connection with your audience is not optional. It's essential to the process of persuasion. Without a connection, you stand little to no chance of influencing your listeners' thoughts, tugging at their emotions, or changing their minds.

Aristotle theorized that a speaker's ability to persuade an audience is based on how well that speaker wields the rhetorical devices of *pathos*, *logos*, and *ethos*. Considered together, these devices form what scholars now call the rhetorical triangle. Let's explore how the rhetorical triangle shows up in the real world.

102 PRESENTATION READY

▶ **Pathos: Emotion—"Yes, that's exactly how I feel."** Pathos speaks to feelings, sentiments, and passions. It's the part of a presentation that uses different kinds of storytelling—music, poetry, narrative—to establish common ground with the audience and elicit specific emotional responses. People are moved to action by how a speaker makes them feel.

▶ **Logos: Logic—"Yes, that makes sense."** Logos appeals to reasoning, deduction, and rationality. It's the part of the presentation that sets forth facts, data, and other evidence that backs up the claims a speaker is making.

▶ **Ethos: Character—"Yes, I trust this person."** Ethos highlights a speaker's status, authority, and ethics. It's the part of a presentation that informs the audience of the speaker's experience, background, and integrity. When you establish credibility in the minds of your listeners, they can feel comfortable trusting you.

Moving forward through this chapter, we will be asking the following three questions:

1. How do speakers connect with audiences emotionally?
2. How do speakers connect with audiences logically?
3. How do speakers establish trust with audiences?

In answering these questions, we will explore real-world scenarios that reflect the challenges and obstacles facing the average presenter.

A Few Real-World Confessions

Our study showed that sales professionals who committed the mistake of failing to create connection with listeners failed to:

MISTAKE #8: FAILURE TO CREATE CONNECTION WITH LISTENERS   103

1. Be authentic and use storytelling to convey emotion and meaning (pathos)
2. Listen and customize content to meet the specific, logic-based needs of the decision maker (logos)
3. Establish credibility while communicating in a warm, friendly manner (ethos)

To avoid making a mistake, we must understand how it manifests in the real world. Let's explore what some of our research participants have said about failing to connect with listeners.

SCENARIO 1

Presenter's Confession. *I'm following the presentation deck and script that my company provides, but it just doesn't seem to be working.*

Listener's Observation. *This presentation just seemed "meh." There was nothing specifically wrong, but nothing great about it either. We just weren't feeling it.*

Solution. Use Storytelling to Convey Authentic Emotion and Meaning (Pathos)

Speakers who don't connect with listeners might be making any number of missteps. They could be just a bit too bland, or they could be trying too hard and come off as overly familiar. They might avoid sharing personal information and give the impression that they're cold and standoffish, or they might share too much. The bottom line is they are not effectively weaving the right amount of pathos—that specific appeal to emotions, sympathetic imagination, beliefs, and values—into their presentations. The presenter could have incorporated personal stories and style in a way that complemented the company script, making the message authentically her own.

PRESENTATION READY

Aristotle believed that persuasion simply does not happen without the presence of emotion, and that the most effective way to transfer emotion from one person to another is through storytelling.

Using Storytelling to Transfer Emotion

Advanced neuroscience has proved Aristotle's thesis. Studies show that the human brain floods with oxytocin when people hear stories that let them experience kindness and trust. Carmine Gallo, an author and instructor at Harvard University, analyzed 500 of the most popular TED Talks of all time and found that stories composed 65 percent of the average speaker's talk. Another 25 percent was devoted to arguments and logic (logos), and 10 percent was spent on establishing credibility, or ethos. "In other words, the winning formula for a popular TED talk is to wrap the big idea in a story," Gallo says.

In the scenario above, the speaker attempted to persuade her listeners, but it sounds as if she lacked the ability to generate any chemistry with the audience. On one hand, she did everything her company trained her to do. She rolled out the charts and data and product highlights one by one, but she paired none of her ideas with the magic of a story. The prospect couldn't point to any one thing she had done wrong, but certainly couldn't pinpoint anything spectacular about her talk.

Sometimes incorporating storytelling means drawing experiences from your personal life and sharing them with an audience. Other times you might start with your audience's story and draw out their current reality and show how you can relate to it. Another option is to share what's known as your "origin story," to lay out the foundation of your personal and professional background, your experience, and your commitment to the work you do.

Whatever path you choose, do not be afraid to use humor. Laughter is universal and has the power to transcend language, culture, and socioeconomic barriers. Any story that demonstrates your understanding of others' circumstances or provokes empathy in others is a good start. It might be a story about how you saved the day for a client, a story that highlights a past failure or moment of awkwardness, or a story that falls somewhere in between those extremes.

Consider this comparison of two sales professionals who worked for a respected and established life insurance company. Both young men believed in their products and services—and were well versed on the company's data, but their styles were different and they approached the work from different perspectives. One man followed the company's manual and slide deck to the letter, always explaining the offerings thoroughly for customers. His sales were steady, and he was doing fine.

The other young man did those things too, but his presentations were infused with a personal story and an undeniable sincerity that stemmed from a family tragedy. A few years earlier, his father had died unexpectedly, and a life insurance policy provided the support his family needed at a very difficult time. The young man knew firsthand what a difference life insurance can make, and when he spoke with customers, his knowledge, gratitude, and authenticity were apparent. He was a true believer and a top producer at the company. Both men had the same training and materials, but by sharing his personal story with customers, the young man who had lost his father was able to differentiate himself in a powerful way.

There is no one correct way to create a connection with an audience. The key is to highlight our shared humanity.

Storytelling and the Visualization Step

While we are on the subject of storytelling, let's revisit the Visualization Step of Monroe's Motivated Sequence in Chapter 2:

> Visualization Step. Invite the audience to imagine themselves in the future, enjoying the benefits that follow the adoption of your plan. Help prospects visualize change. Take them from their present condition to the enhanced lifestyle they envision for themselves. Unless they can see

themselves moving into a new dimension, they won't be convinced that your product or service is necessary.

Notice the direct link between storytelling and visualization when building your persuasive message. Storytelling not only helps presenters create connection; it's also an effective way to help listeners visualize what you are proposing. If listeners can see the benefits coming to life in their minds, they will feel more comfortable about saying yes as you move into the Action Step of your presentation.

SCENARIO 2

Presenter's Confession. *I worked with this company for 20 years and had a great relationship with the previous management team, so when I came in to meet with the new leadership, I felt confident that I would keep them as a client. I was not prepared for the fact that they wanted to go in a very different direction. Looking back, I could have asked more questions about this new team, rather than assuming they would be interested in expanding on what we have already been doing.*

Listener's Observation. *We decided to end our relationship with this vendor after the last presentation. They failed to understand our concerns about their ideas seeming old-school and adapt to our new direction. They kept talking over us rather than pausing to engage or ask questions about our new goals. Bottom line, they had poor acknowledgment of our cues that they needed to shift gears.*

Solution. Listen and Customize Content to Meet the Specific Needs of the Decision Maker (Logos)

In addition to being authentic and genuine with listeners, persuasive speakers must take steps to be aware of their audience's specific

MISTAKE #8: FAILURE TO CREATE CONNECTION WITH LISTENERS   107

circumstances. This awareness lets you choose evidence to back up claims that speak directly to your prospect's challenges and concerns. In situations where you might have a candid conversation with a client about the future of your partnership, this tool requires you to listen at least as much as you speak. And when you listen, it must be with intent. You are listening to your prospects, clients, or customers with the specific goal of handing them a viable, customized solution to their problems. Additionally, you will need to analyze the data, their requests, and any obstacles they're facing to ensure that they know you have heard them and understand their current situation.

In the second scenario, it seems the speaker went in prepared only for what they had previously known. They admit to being biased toward their vision for the company and didn't see the client's desire for something new. This happens more frequently than you might imagine. The presenter didn't stop and listen to the client's evolving needs or realize that the client wanted to move forward under a new relationship. Although the speaker had done their homework, they didn't allow for any expansion beyond the status quo, talked over the client, and did not ask enough questions. As a result, the speaker failed to achieve the burden of logos, disappointed the client, and ultimately lost an opportunity.

How Do Speakers Connect with Listeners Logically?

As mentioned previously, it starts with the careful and layered practice of listening. While there are many kinds of listening, three specific approaches can help you connect with an audience:

- ▶ **Empathetic listening.** The goal is to show mutual concern. You are trying to identify with the other person and see the situation from that person's perspective. During empathetic listening, focus on the other person, not yourself.

108 PRESENTATION READY

▶ **Comprehensive listening.** The goal is to understand the message being shared. Listen actively. This process is active and might include taking notes or keeping track of key points.

▶ **Critical listening.** The goal is to collect and analyze the content you're hearing. You weigh all parts of the message, evaluating the information and making mental judgments to decide for yourself whether the information is valid.

In this listening phase you are gathering the intel so you can apply your analysis and construct the best possible solution, based on the listener's circumstances and perspective.

During this time of listening, speakers will also want to be armed with current, relevant data to respond seamlessly to a client's questions and be mentally prepared for the unexpected. Part of that preparation involves looking around the marketplace to see how you measure up, long before a presentation opportunity. It is your responsibility to find out what makes your competitors unique. Why are they getting sales that could be going to you? Scout out the competition. Do your homework beforehand, because it's hard to build a case on the fly for why you are the better choice if you don't know whom you are up against. Educate yourself about the competition. Is your prospect considering using your competitor's product or service, and if so, why?

SCENARIO 3

Presenter's Confession. *This prospect was right in my wheelhouse. I thought we were a perfect fit for them and at the right price point. I'm not sure what happened.*

Listener's Observation. *The presenter came in overly confident and acted as if they already had the deal. Their style was a bit abrasive and a* *little insulting. They even put down a competitor that we are considering. Something felt off.*

Solution. Establish Credibility While Communicating in a Warm, Friendly Manner (Ethos)

In this scenario, overconfidence bordering on cockiness cost the speaker an opportunity. They did not meet the need of ethos, which speaks to shared values, trust, and credibility—they overstepped badly, coming off as abrasive and insulting. They also showed poor form in putting down a competitor. As a result, the prospect didn't feel comfortable trusting the presenter with their business.

Sales professionals want to share their experience and expertise, but it can feel awkward to talk about yourself. Some people opt out and just don't do it, so they miss out on building a higher level of trust with their prospects. There is a fine line between explaining why you are qualified to speak on a topic and simply being a braggart.

For example, a young woman who worked in a largely male-dominated sector at a company that manufactured boating equipment and generators had never thought to share that she grew up working in a shipyard with her father and brothers. After she explained her background, communicating with her male colleagues became much easier because she had "street cred." It just goes to show that listeners cannot read a speaker's mind. They won't know what you don't tell them.

How Do Speakers Establish Trust with Audiences?

Establishing trust does not happen on its own. It's the result of a wide range of intentional efforts, including sharing your background and bona fides, keeping an open mind about who your listeners are, and speaking in a warm, welcoming manner. There simply is no substitute for likability. Be kind, honest, open, and present. It does not matter how well you know your product or service offering if you aren't connecting with your listeners during the sales process.

In his book *Trusted Leader: 8 Pillars That Drive Results*, Dave Horsager explains the necessity of trust:

> Trust has the ability to accelerate or destroy any business, organization, or relationship. The lower the trust, the more time everything takes, the more everything costs, and the lower the loyalty of everyone involved. Conversely, an environment of trust leads to greater innovation, morale, and productivity.

Horsager argues that trust is quantifiable and has the power to generate dramatic positive results. In his speaking appearances, he often asks audiences, "What's trust got to do with it? Everything!"

Think back for a moment to our last chapter on using visual aids and consider how it relates to this chapter on creating connection with listeners. Creativity is what ultimately makes your message land. Remember that human beings have vastly unique personalities, interests, and skills, and that not every person in your audience will connect with you in the same way. That is why it's critical to blend all three elements—pathos, logos, and ethos—into your presentation.

Here's a peek inside my own process of pairing these concepts to support you as you craft a message that drives connection.

In preparation for a speaking engagement, I set up a visit with my graphic design team to explore an update for the slide I use to explain Aristotle's rhetorical triangle of pathos (emotion), ethos (character/credibility), and logos (logic). I had been using a simple illustration for a while—a heart for pathos, a brain for logos, and a diploma seal for ethos, as seen earlier in this chapter—and I was considering putting a little more creativity into the slide.

I explained this goal to the team and said, "Could you come up with something fresh that would really pop to illustrate these ideas? You're the creative team, so I would love to see what you would do!"

They happily agreed and said they'd get back to me within seven days. And this was the new slide:

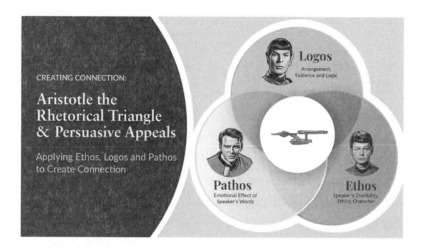

Bursting with excitement, the designers explained the entire image: "Terri, what do you think of this? In the middle, we have the Star Trek *Enterprise*! And Dr. Leonard H. "Bones" McCoy, he represents ethos— don't you think he represents ethos? And get this—Captain James T. Kirk, he was like the heart, so he's pathos. And Spock, he's clearly logos because he's all about logic and no emotion!"

Stunned silence.

"So what do you think, Terri?" they asked.

"This is so . . . interesting!" I answered. "It is interesting. I'm going to use it—but maybe not in the way you think." And here's the thing—they're not wrong. Those descriptions were spot-on.

When I later floated this slide in front of an audience, it did not have across-the-board appeal. Some listeners got it immediately, laughing the whole time. They loved it. Others had no clue what these three men and a spaceship were doing on the screen. And a third group had a vague idea of what it was, but it just didn't land.

And there's the challenge. When you speak to an audience of diverse individuals, you must continually explore how your message will land with them. It's important to note that if your client was a huge Trekkie, this slide would be the perfect vehicle for creating connection.

Now I use both slides to make the point—and it works beautifully.

Conclusion

One reason speakers fail to create connection is that they spend too little time on setting the mood and establishing the common ground that will help bridge the gap between them and their listeners. Remember—people generally tend to gravitate toward those with whom they share interests, outlooks, and values. As this chapter closes the book's section on creativity, make an effort to have fun with this element of expression. It deserves your attention and original thought.

Summary

Mistake #8 is failing to create connection with listeners. It is the inability to establish a genuine and authentic personal and professional bond with an audience or decision maker. It's failing to read the room, understand the prevailing mood, and adjust your presentation accordingly.

- Ancient Greek philosopher Aristotle taught that a speaker's ability to persuade an audience is based on how well that speaker wields the rhetorical devices of pathos, logos, and ethos.
- Pathos speaks to feelings, sentiments, and passions.
- Logos appeals to reasoning, deduction, and rationality.
- Ethos highlights a speaker's status, authority, and ethics.
- Connection drives action. History and data have repeatedly demonstrated that speakers who form a connection with their listeners are more likely to persuade them to listen, change their minds, or decide to act.

▶ **Next Up.** Mistake #9: Distracting Gestures and Body Language

SECTION III
DELIVERY

Delivery includes the elements of your overall performance effort. It features your unique style, movement, personality, and ability to execute effectively.

MISTAKE #9

Distracting Gestures and Body Language

DEFINITION

A speaker's nonverbal expressions, physical behaviors, or movements that can disrupt a listener's attention or concentration. Body language and facial expressions, including issues relating to spatial relationships, can be misinterpreted by the audience and ultimately divert attention from your presentation.

Understanding the Issue of Distracting Gestures and Body Language

In most discussions about mastering the art of persuasive communication, the greatest emphasis is placed on the content of the speaker's message. Content certainly is essential, but the physical act of speaking is equally important. Words and nonverbal movements work in concert to communicate a message. It takes the audience only a few moments to watch, listen, and decide if your facial expressions, tone of voice, and physical movement are reinforcing what's being said or detracting from it. Your entire physical presence—the way you stand, sit, move, and gesture—is expressive and has the power to convey a wide range of meanings. A message is clearest when your nonverbals complement your words, instead of working against them.

118 PRESENTATION READY

Think of those speakers who capture your attention and hold it until their final words have been shared. They bring what they are saying to life by creating "a movie in the mind" and transporting their listeners to another place in time, even if only for a few minutes. If you were to analyze their presentations, you would likely see that their nonverbals consistently align with the messages they are sharing. Even small, subtle movements—choosing to sit or stand, lifting a hand or holding up a single finger in emphasis—are powerful. Whatever the meeting or conversation calls for, these speakers have tapped into a physical presence necessary to communicate their message effectively.

It can be quite easy. Your body naturally wants to gesture. If you have ever been on a hands-free phone call or watched yourself presenting on the playback from a recorded video platform call, you might have noticed yourself gesturing away with no awareness at all. It's typically something that happens instinctively without forethought or specific intention. These mannerisms are a part of your personal communication style, and the more you can harness them to enhance your message, the more you will connect with your audience.

In the State of Sales Presentations research study, participants provided numerous examples of observed behaviors and physical movements that can undermine the effectiveness of a presentation:

- ▶ Pointing a finger at the audience
- ▶ Twirling a strand of hair, pushing up glasses, fiddling with jewelry or tie
- ▶ Playing with keys or pocket change
- ▶ Clicking a pen repeatedly
- ▶ Moving one's hands continuously
- ▶ Pacing restlessly while speaking
- ▶ Standing or sitting with a slouch or sagging shoulders

MISTAKE #9: DISTRACTING GESTURES AND BODY LANGUAGE **119**

- ▶ Making minimal eye contact, making too much eye contact, or failing to make eye contact at all
- ▶ Standing or walking with a stiff, robotlike posture or gait
- ▶ Standing too close to the camera or to an in-person audience

Many of these distracting gestures and behaviors are fueled by nervousness, fear, and lack of preparation. And like every other part of a compelling persuasive talk, creating a strong and engaging physical presence takes awareness and intention.

A Few Real-World Confessions

Our study showed that sales professionals who used distracting gestures and body language failed to (1) have an awareness of their nonverbal communication in a meeting or presentation, (2) be intentional about eye contact, and (3) move with meaning. As with any mistake, to avoid making it, one must understand how it manifests in the real world. Let's explore what some of our research and workshop participants have said about presenters who exhibited distracting gestures and body language.

SCENARIO 1

Presenter's Confession. *I went into the meeting feeling excited for the opportunity but extremely nervous because I was presenting to my organization's senior leadership. It was a hybrid presentation—some people in person and some people watching via a video platform—and on top of that the session was recorded. (Brutal!) When I watched the playback, I was mortified to see I was moving my hands a lot and sometimes my back was to the camera. I seemed a bit hyper. Ugh!*

Listener's Observation. *The presenter has a lot of potential, but we feel they could use a bit of professional polish and coaching to help them with* *their executive presence. The excessive movement and pacing were a little awkward and distracting.*

Solution. Have an Awareness of Nonverbal Communication in a Meeting or Presentation

Most sales professionals can relate to the presenter's confession in this scenario and how the person's nervous energy was expressed physically through excessive gesturing. Whatever environment you are presenting in, it pays to gain awareness of your nonverbal communication. To do this, try the record, review, and refresh approach outlined below. This practice will help you recognize unconscious movements and habits that may be distracting to listeners.

Record

It's impossible to fix a problem that you don't know exists, so you must first gain an awareness of your physicality during a live presentation—your stance and posture, resting facial expressions, hand movements, and over-all bearing. And thanks to smartphones and mobile devices, gathering this kind of personal insight is easier than ever before. Just record yourself delivering your presentation, and then watch the talk with a trusted friend or colleague who is willing to be candid.

Review

While watching yourself speak, act as though you are on a fact-finding mission and strive to objectively identify key problems. Remember that when it comes to distracting gestures and body language, what you don't know can hurt you. Watching yourself speak also provides you with the opportunity to take in what your listeners see and hear. While this isn't the most comfortable or enjoyable exercise, it can be immensely helpful to speakers looking to polish and strengthen their performance.

Here are a few areas to keep an eye on:

Facial Expression

Positive: Relaxed smiles convey friendliness and acceptance.

Negative: Narrowed eyes and a furrowed brow suggest suspicion and unease.

Body Movements

Positive: Hands on hips could express confidence and conviction (use sparingly).

Negative: A bouncing knee indicates nervousness and anxiety.

Hand Gestures

Positive: Graceful, well-timed flourishes convey style and flair.

Negative: Clenched fists and pointed fingers suggest anger.

Instinctual Mannerisms

Positive: When your body takes over and you are actively engaging in a story to bring it to life.

Negative: When it's too much.

Refresh

Once you are clear on what you need to improve, change, or stop doing altogether, it is also important to focus on what you are doing well. Have you ever attended an event where a speaker left you in awe of their eloquence, energy, and timing? They make it look so easy. For a few natural talents out there, it is. For the rest of us—and that's most of us—it takes practice, practice, and more practice. The reality is that most of those speakers you admire have simply put in the work, honing their speaking style, rehearsing specific talks, and ultimately gaining an acute awareness of their own physical presence. When they take to the stage or sit down in front of the camera, they can communicate with an ease and polish that instantly engages their listeners.

SCENARIO 2

Presenter's Confession. *I just didn't know where to look, so I just glanced at the audience from time to time. I felt awkward and didn't want to seem like I was staring, so I kept my eye contact to a minimum.*

Listener's Observation. *The speaker seemed nervous or disconnected and made no real eye contact. It seemed as if they were looking over my head the entire time.*

Solution. Be Intentional About Eye Contact

Eye contact is nonverbal communication that conveys engagement, creates connection, and expresses acknowledgment. It says, "I see you," and it can serve as a source of feedback for a presenter.

Eye contact, however, can present challenges. Some people experience anxiety or feel uncomfortable with looking directly at another person because of lack of confidence or shyness. Others rely too heavily on eye contact, and the effect can be unsettling and a little annoying. It is important to look directly into the eyes of your listeners with ease, whether speaking one-on-one or addressing a group. It gives others the feeling that you are connecting with everyone in the room. If you look over the heads of people in the audience, it's difficult to connect.

In 2016, the *Royal Society Open Science* journal published the first study about what constitutes normal eye contact. Here's the basic takeaway: Count to three. That's the duration of eye contact most people are comfortable with.

Note *We will discuss this further in Chapter 11, but when speaking on a video platform, remember to speak directly into the camera with "soft eyes" as if speaking to a human being who was sitting in the same room with you.*

SCENARIO 3

Presenter's Confession. *When I watched the playback, I was embarrassed to see that I paced back and forth throughout the presentation.*

Listener's Observation. *The speaker paced back and forth. It was distracting and almost annoying and made it difficult to focus on what they were saying.*

Solution. Move with Meaning

Clearly the presenter and the listener saw the same thing. When presenting to an audience, remember that your movements convey meaning. And the more intentional your movement, the better. As the speaker, you want to subtly lead your listeners along the path you are taking. For instance, if you are sitting down, try shifting your weight at the precise moment you make the change to the next major point in your presentation. If you are standing, try taking a few steps to the side as you approach a transition or new topic. When you do this, the audience will refocus their attention and understand, thanks to your nonverbals, that you are moving to a new idea.

A more elaborate option—useful in presentations to larger groups and in larger spaces—is the six-point star method. This exercise teaches you how to align your stance and movement with the six components of your persuasive presentation.

The six-point star method provides nonverbal cues to the audience that you are transitioning from one idea to another. It helps you stay on track and keeps your message moving progressively forward.

Give it a try:

- Start in the center of the room and make your introduction; this is Position 1.
- Take two or three small steps slightly to the right, plant your feet, and deliver your first body point; this is Position 2.
- Walk three or four steps back to the center, plant your feet, and make the second body point of your presentation; this is Position 3.
- Continue three or four steps to the left, plant your feet, and make the third body point of your presentation; this is Position 4.
- Walk slightly ahead and back toward the center of the room, plant your feet, and start your conclusion; this is Position 5.
- Take one or two steps forward, plant your feet, and make your close; this is Position 6.

SIX POINT STAR DIAGRAM
Moving with Transitions

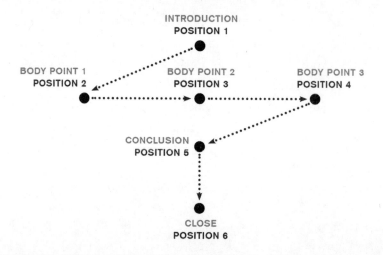

Note: The six-point star method applies when you are presenting to a group. It's not meant to be used in a cramped office or in a one-on-one setting.

Don't Leave Your Nonverbal Communication to Chance

During a presentation, when adrenaline is coursing through your body, the energy must go somewhere, and sometimes it results in odd, even humorous body language. Just as it's poor form to wing it with the spoken content of your message, neither should you wing it with the nonverbals.

Let's go inside the speakers studio to take a closer look at examples of distracting nonverbals and body language:

- ▶ **Hands in your pockets.** No big deal—or is it? When people leave their hands in their front pockets, they inevitably begin to do what we call the "chicken," flapping their arms back and forth as they grow increasingly animated. Now if their collar or shirt is a little tight, it will look very strange because they begin to display almost a rooster effect where they start to move. To say the least, this gesture, while humorous, is terribly distracting for listeners.

- ▶ **One, two, three—kick!** A bright and energetic young sales professional kicked out her leg when she made a significant point. When her fellow team members pointed it out, she was shocked, saying, "I don't know what you're talking about!" Once she reviewed the recording of her presentation, she could clearly see that she looked like a cancan dancer!

- ▶ **Pens and buttons.** One man who had a habit of casually resting his pen on his ear did not realize that he was doing this during his presentations. When he watched himself sitting there with a pen sticking out the side of his head, he was shocked. Another gentleman was so nervous during presentations that he fiddled with the buttons on his shirt. He would repeatedly unbutton his shirt and then button it back up again.

126 PRESENTATION READY

▶ **To bee or not to bee.** A workshop participant told a story about having a bee fly into his ear. He illustrated the point by sticking his finger right where the bee flew in. This gesture was highly effective the first time. But throughout his talk he kept repeating it, to the point of being compulsive. The movement was so distracting that it overshadowed everything he was saying.

▶ **Penguins and spiders.** The "penguin" is keeping one's arms locked straight down on your sides, but still moving one's hands. The "spider" happens when one brings one's palms together but with only the fingertips touching and moving in unison. Both gestures are awkward and distracting.

▶ **The robot.** The robot often shows up in playback sessions. It happens when people move around in a very stiff way as though all their joints need lubricating—sort of like the Tin Man after the rainstorm in *The Wizard of Oz*.

▶ **Oops! Too close.** Don't be Aaron, the annoying "close talker" from the now-famous episode of the classic television show *Seinfeld*. Nobody likes a close talker. Spatial relationships are important to people. It is up to a speaker to allow listeners to set the speaking distance. If a listener invites you closer, then move forward. If not, stand back and respect your listener's personal space.

While we had a little fun here, sharing a few extreme examples from live workshops, the underlying message is clear: You can't depend on others to point out what you are doing wrong. During these workshops, the participants could clearly see their peers' missteps, but did not say anything because they didn't want to hurt anyone's feelings. In general, people don't want to have that awkward conversation, and that's why it's crucial for you to police your own gestures and body language. Take the initiative and watch yourself in action, so you can make corrections. When speakers

MISTAKE #9: DISTRACTING GESTURES AND BODY LANGUAGE 127

leave this aspect of a presentation to chance or a desire to be in the moment, strange and even annoying habits can start to form, and these habits only distract from their ability to connect with listeners.

Gesture with Meaning

Amanda Gorman, the first United States National Youth Poet Laureate, elevated hand gestures to an entirely new level when she delivered her poem "The Hill We Climb" at the inauguration of President Joseph Biden in 2021. Her graceful, perfectly timed movements infused her words with a beautiful energy that captured the attention of everyone who watched. A *Scientific American* profile describes Gorman as "an original" who "shows us that gestures are not mere hand-waving. They can convey images that magnify speech or even add new ideas that are not found in the spoken word." The flutter and flow of her fingertips were in perfect sync with her words.

Gorman's delivery demonstrated how gestures can reveal unspoken ideas, curb misunderstanding, and heighten the meaning and intent of what we say, ultimately leading to more effective communication.

Are there parts of your presentation that might benefit from a few well-placed and rehearsed hand gestures or movements?

Conclusion

Nonverbals are a natural part of a person's speaking style. They are, in fact, an essential part of the way we all communicate with one another. All the people discussed in the examples above knew they were being recorded, and their strange tics and behaviors still happened. Our bodies naturally want to gesture. The key is harnessing that energy and turning it into intentional, well-timed movements that emphasize, enhance, and complement our words.

Summary

Mistake #9 is distracting gestures and body language. It addresses a speaker's nonverbal expressions, physical behaviors, or movements that can disrupt a listener's attention or concentration.

- A presenter's words and nonverbal movements work in concert to communicate a message and direct audience attention.
- Most negative body language is a result of nervousness and lack of preparation.
- To establish the executive presence necessary in most sales presentations, speakers must gain an awareness of their nonverbal communication.
- An effective way to connect with an audience is to be intentional about eye contact.
- As you present, harness your energy and move with meaning.

▶ **Next Up.** Mistake #10: Dressing Inappropriately or Unprofessionally

MISTAKE #10

Dressing Inappropriately or Unprofessionally

DEFINITION
Showing up to a presentation in clothing not suitable for you or the overall occasion; failing to reflect the appropriate intention, brand, culture, atmosphere, or message in clothing choice for that specific situation.

Understanding the Issue of Dressing Inappropriately or Unprofessionally

It's natural for us to think the way we dress is fine, whether we know anything about clothes or not. Some people think dressing is more about function, while others think it's all about style. The bottom line is that both things can be true at the same time. Some of us assume that as long as we aren't wearing shorts to work and a tuxedo to the company picnic, no one will notice or even care. But between the shorts and the tuxedo are countless opportunities to make a poor impression and lose out on an opportunity.

Consider the way you dress for work—are you sending the right message? Whether or not you like it, listeners start assessing your competence within the first few seconds you walk in the door, and much of this interpretation is based on how you look. Before you formally begin to present, they're already making judgments about your credibility and the likelihood of doing business with you. How you are dressed has a notable effect on those judgments.

130 PRESENTATION READY

Data has supported this idea for decades, and yet most of us have been guilty of showing up somewhere, at one time or another, dressed inappropriately. And when you become aware of the mistake, it's a terribly uncomfortable feeling. This misstep can tank your confidence at a time when you need to be at your best.

Wearing inappropriate dress can also have a negative impact on first impressions and the connection you are trying to make with your listeners, particularly if you are following someone else who happens to be well dressed.

For many professionals, attire is often guided or even dictated by an organization's official policies and rules. Yet even in companies with established dress codes, there are discrepancies between how employees dress for work and how their supervisors think they should dress. To be sure, it's a difficult subject to broach, and many managers feel it's almost too personal to tackle. They also don't want employees to feel pressured into having to spend money on clothes and are reluctant to say anything to their associates about inappropriate dress. This only perpetuates the problem.

In the State of Sales Presentations research study, the mistake of dressing inappropriately or unprofessionally was highly noted as being observed in other presenters but self-reported in lower numbers. The mistake was also found to have a negative impact on wanting to work with someone. Study and workshop participants provided numerous examples of dressing inappropriately or unprofessionally, including:

- ▶ "The representative looked a bit disheveled and did not make the best impression."

- ▶ "Sales rep was wearing a hoodie for the sales call—just because we are meeting virtually doesn't mean they shouldn't show up professionally, right?"

- ▶ "Speaker looked like they were going to a party, not a business meeting."

A Few Real-World Confessions

The results showed that sales professionals who committed this mistake failed to (1) dress appropriately for the meeting or opportunity whether in person, virtual, or hybrid, and (2) dress to boost confidence in their overall presence and to adopt a strategic mindset.

As with any mistake, to avoid making it, one must understand how it manifests in the real world. Let's explore what some of our research participants have said about the mistake of wearing inappropriate dress.

SCENARIO 1

Presenter's confession. *I confess that I haven't been dressing up for my virtual presentations in the same way I would for in-person meetings. I work from home, and nobody really dresses up in my industry anymore.*

Listener's Observation. *The presenter was dressed a bit too informally, and it was hard to take them seriously.*

Solution. Dress Appropriately for the Opportunity, Whether the Meeting is In Person, Virtual, or Hybrid

> If you want to make it on Wall Street or Main Street,
> pay careful attention to the clothes you wear
> and the visual impact you have on others.
> —NIDO R. QUBEIN

If your job is client facing, it's crucial to dress for the occasion of meeting with a prospect or listener, and that might well be different from how you dress on other days. In today's diverse markets, professional dress is not an absolute. It can change and morph according to the industry, the culture, and the nature of the meeting. For example, if you are calling on a company within the construction industry and your meeting is taking place at a build site, you may need to dress for that environment—in safe and sturdy shoes and a hard hat—but still look sharp. If your prospect works in the arts and entertainment industry, there might be room to dress more fashionably or reveal some of your own personal style. If you are heading into the financial services sector, a more conventional look is still your best bet.

The worst sins of inappropriate dress, of course, include those old-school notions you may have heard about when you were growing up: wrinkled clothes that look like you slept in them, unpressed suits with no creases in the trousers, colors that clash, clothes that are grossly out of style, shoes that are inappropriate for your activity—the wrong style or color—or shoes that are scuffed up and worn down at the heels, ties that are too wide, and too many accessories.

Keep in mind that appropriate professional dress is a presentation-ready priority. With the rise of work-from-home environments, it is somewhat amusing, and even a little endearing, to do business remotely in your pajamas or yoga pants with a messy ponytail, saying things like, "Gosh, I'm sorry. I'm just a hot mess today!" However, if you are sitting on your bed making presentations to customers and business partners, it's time to level up. Even if you are working remotely, you should strive to dress as if you are meeting in person. After all, your home office is an extension of your formal business office space, and the way you dress still speaks to your work ethic, integrity, and attentiveness. The amusing part of this discussion is how many people confess that they still show up on virtual calls adopting the business-at-the-top-and-casual-at-the-bottom look. They wear sweat pants and a collared dress shirt. It's a risk, as you never know what the camera might reveal.

MISTAKE #10: DRESSING INAPPROPRIATELY OR UNPROFESSIONALLY **133**

SCENARIO 2

Presenter's Confession. *I just didn't think it was that big of a deal. Nobody in my industry wears a suit and tie anymore, and I have heard that it's completely acceptable to dress down these days. That said, I do carry myself differently—with more confidence—when I wear a suit.*

Listener's Observation. *Maybe our company is a bit traditional, but we still adhere to a professional dress code. We notice when a partner doesn't dress in a way that blends with our culture or inspires them to carry themselves with an air of confidence.*

Solution. Dress to Boost Confidence in Your Overall Presence and Adopt a Strategic Mindset

We have all heard the phrase "dress to impress," but what if you not only dressed to impress, but also started dressing to express? Dress to show customers, prospects, and partners that you are serious, prepared, polished, and capable. One of the best reasons to pay close attention to your clothes is that it tells your audience you are honored to be there, all-in, and eager to win their time or business.

Think of a time when you dressed up to look your absolute best at an industry awards ceremony or a colleague's retirement reception. You did that as a sign of respect for the event host as well as for your fellow guests. As a result, your presence and appearance subtly indicated your knowledge of the social graces, while also sending a message of gratitude.

When you are uncertain of what to wear to a specific business event, do not hesitate to ask someone in the know. Take the guesswork out of it and clarify what kind of attire would be most appropriate. Even when it's a casual affair, it's best to take it up a notch to look as if you put some effort into your appearance.

Setting the Right Tone

The way you dress to deliver a presentation not only sets an important tone with your listeners, it can also increase your own confidence in your abilities. That confidence can, in turn, lead to a sharper awareness, higher energy, and an overall better performance. The late, legendary syndicated radio news talk show host Paul Harvey always wore a suit and tie with all the appropriate accessories when doing his radio show. During an episode of *The Larry King Show*, King asked Harvey why he was always so dressed up for his radio show when, obviously, no one could see him. He responded, "I can't explain why. But I do know that the times I've tried to go casual . . . something is sacrificed."

Larry said, "You're not as good?"

Paul responded, "I don't know if good is the word. I can't put my finger on it. But I do know something is missing."

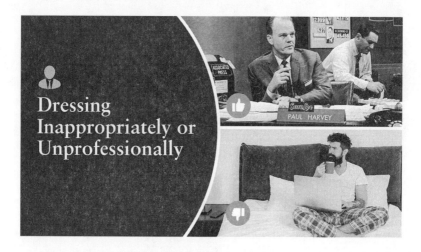

Suits for Self-Confidence

The organization Dress for Success provides a classic example of how dress can impact an individual's attitude and bearing. Dress for Success was founded by Nancy Lublin, a second-year law student who received a

MISTAKE #10: DRESSING INAPPROPRIATELY OR UNPROFESSIONALLY **135**

$5,000 inheritance from her great-grandfather in 1996 and resolved to put it to good use. Partnering with three nuns in her area, she identified a crucial unmet need and started the nonprofit in the basement of a Manhattan church that same year. Dress for Success provides women with professional clothes and the guidance they need for an interview. When they find employment, they can return for the apparel and accessories they will need to enter the workforce. Companies ranging from shoe stores to cosmetics retailers help with donated products.

According to Dress for Success, women who received suits expressed a tremendous boost in their self-confidence when they were dressed professionally for a job interview, which helped generate better outcomes. Lublin said, "They walk out of here really cocky and confident, and that's the point."

Today Dress for Success has expanded to 143 cities in 23 countries and has helped more than 1.3 million women move closer to self-sufficiency.

Cost of Dressing Well

Although dressing well can represent a small financial investment for many people, it's an investment in yourself and your career. But that investment doesn't have to break the bank, because you don't have to spend a lot of money on clothes to look neat, professional, and attractive. Many people dress extremely well without ever buying anything new. They frequent consignment stores to find affordable high-end brands. Online wardrobe rental is another option. These services are fun and flexible, allowing customers to try before they buy and budget for specific items they will want or need in the future.

If you have a special event and you don't want to buy an expensive outfit, borrow one from a friend or relative. That person might be happy to lend you a blouse, shirt, or tie. You are only going to wear it once, anyway, and most friends will want to help you out. Just remember to give it back after the obligatory trip to a reputable dry cleaner. Dress so that every day you meet with a prospect, you feel like you are ready to present your best self.

My Family Set the Stage

When I was growing up, my mom and dad would take my sister and me to see our grandparents on Sundays, and when we visited Nana and Pop Pops, we had best be "dressed like ladies." As a kid, it was a bit annoying because I usually wanted to be in play clothes, but the rule was nonnegotiable. My grandparents were both born and raised in England, my grandmother was a very poised woman, and my grandfather knew how to wear a suit as he was a tailor for JC Penney's until the day he retired.

My grandparents were not wealthy people, but they were always beautifully dressed, well pressed, and they were the classiest people I've ever known. I learned from my grandparents a long time ago—class has nothing to do with money. This early experience taught me at a young age the importance of dressing with the occasion in mind.

Establishing Your Own Style

An increasing number of people subscribe to the idea of wearing the same thing every day. For some, it is part of embracing a more minimalist way of life, reducing waste, saving money, and avoiding the stress of managing an ever-changing wardrobe.

For others, it's about creating an iconic look that speaks to your personal brand. Consider late Apple cofounder Steve Jobs, who famously wore a black mock turtleneck, blue jeans, and New Balance tennis shoes every day. The simple uniform was his way of reducing decision fatigue by prioritizing his brainpower and giving himself one fewer decision to make each day. We're not all Steve Jobs. Still there is something to be said for wearing an outfit that transitions well from day to night and between a wide range of business opportunities.

Is There a Best Color to Wear for a Business Presentation?

Is there a best color to wear for an important meeting or presentation? Gray, blue, black, red? In most business settings, navy blue is a solid option. It has been said that "True navy blue can go anywhere" and "is a universal color of understated authority." Although conventional, it's a multipurpose choice that easily bridges the gap between daytime and evening meetings.

Clothing color can convey a wide range of messages, including confidence, intelligence, and approachability. It can also provoke specific responses, such as excitement, laughter, or curiosity, in an audience. To determine which colors, shades, and hues complement your individual attributes, a color consultant could be helpful.

Seven Tips to Help You Avoid Dressing Inappropriately for Your Next Meeting or Opportunity

1. Make sure your clothes look clean, pressed, and coordinated.
2. Put a bit of effort into it. Get to know the decision makers' culture, and dress appropriately for the type of meeting you are attending.
3. Be comfortable and look sharp enough to feel self-confident.
4. Whether the clothes are new or old, they must fit well. Get to know a good tailor or dressmaker.
5. Clean and polish your shoes.
6. Choose tasteful accessories that complement your clothes. Don't overdo it unless that's your style—and then own it!
7. Coordinate your colors. If you don't know the rules, consider working with a clothing consultant. When in doubt, go with the tried-and-true navy blue.

Summary

Mistake #10 is dressing inappropriately or unprofessionally: showing up to a presentation in clothing that's not suitable for you or the overall occasion; failing to reflect the appropriate intention, brand, culture, atmosphere, or message in clothing choice for that specific situation.

- The way you dress for a meeting or presentation can positively or negatively impact the outcome.

- Dress for the occasion—and that might well be different from how you ordinarily dress.

- The way you dress to deliver a presentation not only sets an important tone with your listeners, but can also increase your own confidence in your abilities.

- Clothing color can convey a wide range of messages, including credibility, intelligence, and approachability.

- Dressing well may require a small financial investment at first, but it is one that will pay you back many times over.

▶ **Next Up.** Mistake #11: Technology or Demonstration Failures

MISTAKE #11

Technology or Demonstration Failures

DEFINITION

Experiencing an equipment or software malfunction—a product or service that fails to perform correctly during a presentation. Can include good old-fashioned human error in executing a demonstration or utilizing technology effectively.

Understanding the Issue of Technology or Demonstration Failures

Chances are you have experienced a live demonstration that truly delivered on the *wow* factor. By the end of the presentation, you could genuinely see, touch, hear—maybe even taste—the product, service, feature, or outcome. When it all came together, the presenter might even have said, "So great, it speaks for itself!" Sounds reasonable and quite simple in theory, but it is not always so easy to accomplish. The burden of the live demo is that the proof is in the pudding: "Show me it does what you say it can do." If it does, great. If it doesn't, you must make up a lot of ground in a short amount of time.

In the world of sales presentations, countless hours are spent to "bring the show" and roll out a fabulous experience. Unfortunately, if your tools don't work, the connection fails, or the recipe doesn't taste right, the opportunity is lost, and you are unable to move things forward.

139

140 PRESENTATION READY

In the State of Sales Presentations research study, and in follow-up workshops and interviews, participants told us about two kinds of behavior they'd observed around this mistake: (1) system, product, and service failures and (2) simple human error. These problems happened in a variety of presentation formats, including in person, virtual, and hybrid.

System, Product, and Service Failures

- ▶ "The presenter failed to connect with Wi-Fi or integrate with our on-site system."
- ▶ "Oh wow! They came in to show us how _____ worked, and it completely froze up in the middle of the presentation."
- ▶ "I just think their presentation required too much data and bandwidth, and we couldn't receive it properly on our end."
- ▶ "During a demonstration on how to fold a stroller, it got stuck and a piece broke off, leaving the product looking cheaply made and difficult to use."

Simple Human Error

- ▶ "The presenter forgot to add one of the key ingredients when demonstrating a beverage maker. The result was the worst-tasting drink I have had in a while."
- ▶ "When their system went down, the speaker became terribly flustered and didn't have the skill set to rally and keep going."
- ▶ "They spent way too much time showing us the pieces and parts of how the product was put together. I don't care about the sausage making—just show me it can work!"
- ▶ "It was a virtual meeting, and the team's delivery was terrible. The entire time they spoke to the product, not to us."

As you can see, technology and demonstration failures can play out whether you are presenting in person, on a video-based platform, or in some combination of the two. The trick is to become competent at presenting in all three formats. One important reminder is that "client facing" does not necessarily mean physically in person.

Art, Science, and Technology Working Hand in Hand

While the technology behind videoconferencing has certainly existed for a while now, its use has become universally adopted—and more importantly, expected—in private homes, small businesses, large corporations, and government agencies.

What does that mean for sales professionals who dislike the video call? It's time to embrace it. Videoconferencing gives presenters a lot of options, such as allowing them to share a big-picture idea in a remote call so that they might focus on the most salient issues for their listeners when they do meet in person. It's also a smart way to get in front of the most sought-after listeners who are challenging to meet with in person—especially if there are multiple decision makers in various locations. Or it can be an opportunity to meet with prospects and customers across the globe to manage an entire transaction, bypassing the time and cost of international travel.

Ultimately, virtual meetings can't provide all the benefits of face-to-face meetings, but they are scalable and can save you and your prospects time and money. Some people simply feel awkward and uncomfortable using this technology. A common confession is, "I have been presenting for years. Why is this so difficult?" The reason it's daunting is because we are merging the art of presenting, the science of selling, and the modern tools of technology. It's a lot to juggle all at once.

In fact, for some individuals, learning to master this technology is a lot like learning to drive a manual transmission, or stick-shift, automobile after years of driving an automatic. David Amaral, who owns the digital design company Phantom Design, explains it this way:

> You're suddenly trying to navigate the road in front of you while engaging the clutch and shifting gears, and it's awkward. Invariably, there's a stoplight—or even worse, a stoplight on a hill—and you might stall and then start to panic. You want to give up, but you must be able to drive! Time after time, you get behind the wheel, and it's scary and frustrating. Until it isn't. The more you drive, the more you get the hang of a standard transmission, and it starts to be fun.

This is where so many of us are with video call platforms. We'd better figure this out, or we won't get where we need to go.

A Few Real-World Confessions: System, Product, and Service Failures

As with any mistake, to avoid making it, one must understand how it manifests in the real world. Let's explore what some of our research participants have said about technology and demonstration failures.

SCENARIO 1

Presenter's Confession. *Everything worked great yesterday, but I didn't double-check my video platform system again before going live today, and several things did not work properly.*

Listener's Observation. *It didn't inspire confidence when the speaker's video presentation failed. It gave us cause to pause.*

Solution. Prepare Adequately and Use an Equipment and Video Call Checklist to Cover Your Bases and Set Yourself Up for Success

MISTAKE #11: TECHNOLOGY OR DEMONSTRATION FAILURES **143**

Simple Video & Tech-Ready Checklist (see form on page 145)

Set the Stage

- ▶ Location: Where is the best space for your setup?
- ▶ Ambience: What mood are you trying to convey?
- ▶ Background: Does your background encourage connection with the audience?

Lighting

- ▶ Soft, diffused lighting is best. The light should be behind the camera, shining on your face.
- ▶ Watch for dim lighting, harsh shadows, and bright light shining through open blinds.
- ▶ Invest in an LED light or small desk lamp with diffusion to create soft light.

Your In-Person and/or On-Screen Image

- ▶ Look your best—makeup, hair, and clothes. It's showtime!
- ▶ If you are going on camera, set the camera just above eye level and tilt slightly downward. Stack your laptop or tablet on books or boxes to achieve the height you need.
- ▶ Make virtual eye contact by looking directly into the camera, not at yourself on the screen.
- ▶ Center your head and torso and take up most of the frame.
- ▶ Remember you are the star. Don't let visual aids overshadow your message.

144 PRESENTATION READY

Sound

- ▶ Speak clearly and make sure that it's easy to hear you.
- ▶ Upgrade to a high-quality microphone to get better overall sound.
- ▶ Conduct a microphone check with a friend or colleague to get feedback on your vocal tone and clarity.
- ▶ Control background noise, particularly when working from home. Consider using noise-blocking apps.

Gear

- ▶ Determine if your computer is prepared for optimum delivery based on your needs.
- ▶ Use Wi-Fi, wired/hardline, or both.
- ▶ Use a high-quality webcam to improve visual image, warmth, resolution, and depth.
- ▶ Make sure bandwidth and network latency are at optimum capabilities for your needs. (Bandwidth is the amount of data that can be transferred from one point to another within a network in a specific amount of time. Network latency is the amount of time it takes for data to go from the source to its destination. It is measured in milliseconds. The closer your latency is to zero, the better.)

Plan B

- ▶ In case of system failure, what is your backup plan?

Simple Video & Tech Ready Checklist

Set the Stage

☐ Location – Where is the best space for your setup?
☐ Ambience – What mood are you trying to convey?
☐ Background – Does your background encourage connection with the audience?

Lighting

☐ Soft, diffused lighting is best, should be behind the camera, and shining on your face.
☐ Watch for dim lighting, harsh shadows, and bright light shining through open blinds.
☐ Invest in a LED light, or small desk lamp with diffusion to create soft light.

Your In-Person and/or On-Screen Image

☐ Look your best—makeup, hair, and clothes. It's showtime!
☐ If you're going on camera, set the camera just above eye level and tilt slightly downward. (Stack your laptop or tablet on books or boxes to achieve the height you need.)
☐ Make virtual eye contact by looking directly into the camera, not at yourself on the screen.
☐ Center your head and torso and take up most of the frame.
☐ Remember you are the star. Don't let your visual aids overshadow your message.

Sound

☐ Speak clearly and make sure that it's easy to hear you.
☐ Upgrade to a high-quality microphone to get better overall sound.
☐ Conduct a microphone check with a friend or colleague to get feedback on your vocal tone and clarity.
☐ Control background noise, particularly when working from home.
☐ Consider using noise-blocking apps.

Gear

☐ Determine if your computer is prepared for optimum delivery.
☐ Use Wi-Fi, wired/hardline, or both.
☐ Use a high-quality webcam to improve visual image, warmth, resolution, and depth of picture.
☐ Make sure bandwidth and network latency are at optimum capabilities for your needs. (Bandwidth is measured as the amount of data that can be transferred from one point to another within a network in a specific amount of time. Network latency is the amount of time it takes for data or a request to go from the source to its destination. It is measured in milliseconds, and the closer your latency is to zero, the better.)

Plan B

☐ In case of system failure, what is your backup plan?

146 PRESENTATION READY

SCENARIO 2

Presenter's Confession. *I was in the middle of a video call presentation from home when my wireless router stopped functioning. I called my prospects using my cell phone to keep things moving forward, but it was an awkward recovery.*

Listener's Observation. *The speaker's connection was lost, and there was radio silence for a while before they called back on a cell phone. With no visuals, it was difficult to fully grasp their message.*

Solution. Have a Low-Tech or No-Tech Backup Plan in the Event of Total Equipment Breakdown

It happens to everyone. Even the most seasoned veterans have experienced tech or demo failures. Elon Musk and Bill Gates have had demonstration failures—bulletproof glass shattered by a rock and the blue screen of death, respectively—at critical moments. If it can happen to them, it can happen to anyone, so it's not a matter of if, it's a matter of when. When it happens to you, what matters is being prepared.

Let's imagine the previous scenario, where your Wi-Fi signal is weak or crashes altogether. First, if you routinely have video-based calls at home, set up your system with a hardline if you can. In a home where multiple people access the internet, a hardline is a safety net and can give you a more consistent signal than Wi-Fi offers. The other people in your home can use the Wi-Fi while you use the hardline. This alone eliminates a lot of challenges.

Second, it can be helpful to email a simple outline of your most salient talking points, with room for notes and your contact information, to your participants before your meeting. If you must pivot to a good old-fashioned phone call, at least your handout will keep things flowing and on track.

This strategy is just as effective in a hybrid or in-person situation. A seasoned professional was hired to give a presentation to a large firm at a management briefing in New York City. The organization specifically

MISTAKE #11: TECHNOLOGY OR DEMONSTRATION FAILURES   **147**

requested that she conform to their corporate style for presentation slides and templates.

Just before she went on, the main system crashed. The meeting room was thrown into confusion, and the tech team announced that the system was down for the duration of the morning. But she was cool as can be. After a short, unscheduled break, the tech team got the system up and running, and she proceeded to deliver her talk. Forty-five minutes into her two-hour presentation, the system crashed again—this time for good. But the woman did not panic, because she had the foresight to make sure that everyone in the audience had been given a printed copy of her outline. She carried on—almost seamlessly—with her talk, and her client was extremely impressed.

Small Challenge, Big Recovery

In the event of any kind of tech failure, don't be afraid to change course and improvise. Consider the gentleman who was hosting a lunch-and-learn program from his home office when his laser pointer malfunctioned. He desperately needed a pointer for his presentation, and in a moment of brilliance, he had an idea. During the break he ran upstairs and grabbed his son's Star Wars lightsaber and used that as his pointer. The problem was solved, and the audience loved it.

Sometimes keeping things simple is the best strategy, not to mention that listeners always appreciate a quick recovery. Ask yourself what you would do if your system were to go down in the middle of your presentation, and make sure you are prepared to continue with a plan B.

A Few Real-World Confessions: Simple Human Error

SCENARIO 1

Presenter's Confession. *I developed a great vibe of rapport with the people right in front of me in the conference room, but I completely forgot the online participants were even there. I didn't interact with them virtually or even acknowledge their presence, and I lost their attention. I should have taken steps to customize a hybrid talk to reach both audiences.*

Listener's Observation. *The speaker was engaging, but they were entirely focused on the in-person audience and didn't seem to realize they had a sizable group of online participants. After a while, I lost interest because it was clear they weren't even trying to keep our attention.*

Solution. Prepare a Hybrid Presentation That Connects with Online Listeners as Well as In-Person Audience Members

Technological advancements are rapidly changing the way sales presentations look and sound. Newer tools of communication allow entire teams of professionals to reach farther and faster as they share their messages with listeners down the street, on the opposite coast, and across the globe. But no amount of sophisticated technology will ever supplant the necessity of creating a genuine connection with listeners. Connection—in all its forms—is still what drives persuasion.

But how does forging that connection change when an increasing number of listeners are online participants? How are the needs of those remote audience members—who don't have the benefit of sharing physical space with a speaker—different? What do they need to see and hear to feel truly seen and heard by a speaker? These are all questions you should consider.

MISTAKE #11: TECHNOLOGY OR DEMONSTRATION FAILURES **149**

Many new tools are at your disposal to help you visually interact with a remote audience. These include polls, participant Q&A sessions, chat features, virtual breakout rooms for small-group interactions, and more. These vary depending on the platform you use and your organization's protocol, but they do make a difference.

Visually Acknowledge the Remote Audience

Maintaining eye contact with your remote participants is vital in hybrid scenarios. Eye contact is an expressive, connecting element in persuasive speaking. Whether you are presenting one-on-one, in a small office, or in a large conference room, eye contact conveys attention, engagement, and appreciation. When that eye contact must happen via a video-based platform, speakers must work even harder to stay vigilant and recognize their off-site participants. Here are some best practices to remember during your next hybrid presentation:

- ▶ Don't sit or stand too close to the camera. Imagine your frame positioning much like that of a television newscaster. About waist high is optimal.

- ▶ Look directly at your in-person audience, and be sure to gaze regularly into the camera to connect with your online participants as well.

- ▶ Check eyeglasses for reflections that can distract online viewers. It might help to get a simple LED instead of a halogen light to reduce reflection and lighting issues.

- ▶ If it's an option, partner with an assistant to manage your online interaction with the remote audience.

SCENARIO 2

Presenter's Confession. *My extensive multimedia presentation was scheduled immediately following the lunch break, and all the cables, tablets, and screens were set up and in place. The IT staff dimmed the lights, and I jumped right in, but at the end, when the lights came up, it was obvious that quite a few people had fallen asleep. It was awkward and discouraging, and I wasn't sure how to proceed.*

Listener's Observation. *The speaker's presentation looked sophisticated and engaging, but it just could not compete with full stomachs and a darkened, air-conditioned room. Many in the audience nodded off or outright snoozed through the talk and probably couldn't recall the major talking points. It was just poor planning and unfortunate timing.*

Solution. Conduct a Performance Check and Practice Your Presentation in Advance

Great music and dazzling visuals in your presentation won't matter much if you lose the attention of your audience. In this scenario, conducting a run-through beforehand could have shown the speaker that a cool, dark conference room was far more conducive to napping than to listening, especially for an extended period of time. Consider both "lights down" and "lights up" strategies and the incorporation of one or two activities to generate audience engagement to help maintain your connection with listeners.

SCENARIO 3

Presenter's Confession. *When the equipment failed to perform, it really threw me off. I lost focus and failed to get back on track.*

Listener's Observation. *The speaker really got flustered and didn't have the skill set to keep going when their system went down.*

MISTAKE #11: TECHNOLOGY OR DEMONSTRATION FAILURES **151**

Solution. Handle Malfunctions or Demonstration Challenges
with Finesse and Professionalism

The show must go on! Don't worry if you have been flustered in the past
when things have gone awry. That's okay. Next time it will be better. It
really comes down to practice and having the confidence that no matter
what happens, you can make things work.

All tech tools require specific training to execute with ease and flow.
Not knowing how to use equipment properly in conjunction with your
presentation can waste both money and time. Knowing the appropriate
shortcuts as well as when to use them can be the difference between making and losing a sale.

The good news is, when things work properly, it can be dazzling! Don't
let little mishaps discourage you from using technology or demonstrations in your presentations. Just do the homework and preparation. And
get your head in the game by visualizing a successful outcome. Imagine the
following:

- ▶ The machinery works, the sample tastes or smells amazing, and
  the output generates the optimal response.

- ▶ Videos play on cue with perfect sound and impeccable quality.

- ▶ Virtual reality headsets and experiences immerse the listener into
  a specific scenario.

- ▶ Slides and pictures add the perfect finishing touch to wrap up
  your talk.

Dare We Say Pivot!

As the accurate and sometimes overused saying goes, it's time to pivot!
Despite the risks of technology and demonstration failure, it's worth the
effort. Consider the example of the middle-school science teacher who

had only ever worked in a well-equipped classroom. Suddenly he had to start teaching students remotely. Gathering a few key pieces of technology, he transformed his garage into a surprisingly effective laboratory. With careful planning, unfettered creativity, and numerous backup plans, this teacher was able to engage his students and keep them moving forward through their curriculum.

It wasn't always easy or smooth. Throughout the process, he experienced many setbacks. That's what happens. Setbacks are normal. He learned to slog through frustrating errors as well as tech failures that were outside his control. In the end, he was able to adapt and even innovate, eventually creating an incredibly valuable platform for presenting to his audience.

How can you pivot to level up your skills and increase your opportunities?

Any time presenters incorporate visual aids, equipment, or technology into their talks, they up the stakes a bit, for better or worse. When it works, it can transform a presentation and help you make amazing connections with an audience. Of course, with more moving parts comes the potential for more chaos, and speakers risk problems and malfunctions that they wouldn't face by relying solely on their oral skills.

You can't let that uncertainty and increased risk keep you from expanding and improving your presentations. The best approach is to be prepared for as many unexpected pitfalls as you can anticipate.

Summary

Mistake #11 is technology or demonstration failures: experiencing an equipment or software malfunction—a product or service that fails to perform correctly—during a presentation.

- Issues fall into two distinct categories: (1) system, product, and service failures and (2) simple human error.

- Be prepared for hybrid presentations that connect with online listeners as well as in-person audience members.

- Review the Simple Video & Tech Ready Checklist, and consider creating your own more customized version. Then take the time to use it.

- Handle malfunctions and challenges with finesse and professionalism.

- Low-tech backup tip: Provide your listeners with a printed copy of your presentation outline that includes room for notes and your contact information.

- Set up early, check the equipment in the actual setting, and do a walk-through to make any necessary last-minute adjustments.

▶ **Next Up.** Mistake #12: Verbal Missteps

MISTAKE #12

Verbal Missteps

DEFINITION
Using language that is distracting, confusing, or inappropriate, calling a speaker's delivery skills into question. Examples include repeating filler words such as "you know," using too much industry jargon or too many acronyms, making off-color jokes or offensive cultural references, mumbling, talking too fast, or having an off-putting personal style.

Understanding the Issue of Verbal Missteps

The way a person verbally communicates signals an immediate demonstration of professional competency. As listeners, we draw a correlation of credibility of an individual's ability to lead or execute with the way the person speaks and presents. Even though most of us have been speaking since we were two years old, very little attention is paid to consistently improving upon this skill later in life. When an individual is articulate, is well spoken, or "has a way with words," it's attractive. For a lucky few, this ability comes naturally, but for most people, speaking well is a learned skill that must be developed and refined over time through study, awareness, and trial and error.

This chapter might well trigger thoughts of George Bernard Shaw's 1913 play *Pygmalion*, which turned into the beloved 1956 musical *My Fair Lady*. The play tells the story of pompous phonetics professor Henry

Higgins, who is convinced of his ability to transform a cockney working-class girl into a cultured lady of high society. His subject turns out to be the scrappy Eliza Doolittle, who agrees to elocution lessons to improve her job prospects. The struggle that ensues is as poignant as it is hilarious:

Eliza Doolittle: The rine in spine sties minely in the pline.
Professor Henry Higgins: [*sighs*] The rain in Spain stays mainly in the plain.
Eliza Doolittle: Didn't ah sy that?
Professor Henry Higgins: No, Eliza, you didn't "sy" that; you didn't even "say" that. Now every night before you get into bed, where you used to say your prayers, I want you to say, "The rain in Spain stays mainly in the plain" fifty times. You'll get much further with the Lord if you learn not to offend His ears.

While *My Fair Lady* offers exaggerated examples, it certainly goes to the heart of this chapter—the power of verbal missteps to undermine a speaker's credibility, momentum, and confidence. Eliza is a lovely, spirited young woman, but her coarse vocabulary and unrefined accent are holding her back—and she knows it. It's this awareness that motivates Eliza to take the initiative and endure the uncomfortable process of learning from Professor Higgins, who isn't always the nicest teacher. But under his tutelage, she learns to speak beautifully, which opens her life to a new realm of possibilities and opportunities.

> *Note* *Accents are fabulous! Don't worry about your accent. It is most often an asset, part of your style—just be aware of pronunciation, word usage, and clarity.*

A Few Real-World Observations and Insights

In the State of Sales Presentations research study, participants provided multiple examples of behaviors relating to the mistake of verbal missteps. Particularly interesting was that participants consistently noted verbal missteps in others but not in themselves—until they watched or listened to a playback of their own presentations. As a result, this chapter will reflect their observations instead of confessions as in previous chapters. The study participants were often unaware of their own behavior until it was right in front of their faces and then were truly shocked by what they were hearing and seeing. When the study participants stepped back and viewed their performances through the eyes of listeners, they were able to analyze what they said and did during their own presentations and what they heard and witnessed in their colleagues' talks.

Common issues relating to the mistake of verbal missteps fell into six categories:

1. Word redundancy and use of filler words
2. Too much industry jargon or acronyms
3. Inappropriate language or references
4. Verbal clarity issues
5. Rate, speed, and volume issues
6. Personal style issues

As with any mistake, to avoid making it, one must understand how it manifests in the real world. Let's explore these common problem areas and solutions.

It's important to understand that the key to avoiding and recovering from verbal missteps starts with gaining awareness. Take the time to record and listen to or watch your performance in playback. Ask yourself if you are speaking and presenting in a way

that enhances your credibility. Pay attention to what words you use, how you use them, and how they land among listeners, and then self-assess.

Observation #1: Word Redundancy and Use of Filler Words

- ▶ "Too much repetition."
- ▶ "Too wordy."
- ▶ "Too many unintelligent connector words such as 'you know' and 'like' and 'um'."
- ▶ "Excessive, unnecessary talking resulting in a presentation taking much longer than necessary."

Solutions

- ▶ **Expand your vocabulary.** If you're in a word rut, pick up any book or online resource designed to improve vocabulary, diction, and fluency. Don't be afraid to consult a thesaurus, which is an excellent tool in combatting repetition and broadening your personal lexicon. Another option is to utilize websites that check your grammar and vocabulary usage.
- ▶ **Pause and breathe.** Usually when speakers use words like "um," "ah," "like," or "you know," it's because their brain is trying to catch up with what they are trying to say. Instead of filling that space with a word, fill it with a beat, a moment of time, a breath. It's okay to pause while you find the correct word. It might feel like forever for you, but it doesn't feel that way for the listener.

Observation #2: Too Much Industry Jargon or Acronyms

- ▶ "Didn't explain acronyms."

MISTAKE #12: VERBAL MISSTEPS   **159**

- ▶ "The speaker didn't establish common language."

- ▶ "Failure to tailor word choice to the audience."

- ▶ "Too much jargon such as phrases like 'baked-in,' 'my two cents,' and 'deep dive'."

- ▶ "The speaker wasn't familiar with or fluent in our corporate lingo."

Solutions

- ▶ **Explain acronyms.** Don't let your talk become a messy pot of alphabet soup. Explain acronyms before you use them; it's fine to continue using them after that. For example, at a National Speaker's Association event, one would say NSA after saying National Speaker's Association, for clarity and to avoid confusion with the National Security Agency. We are professional speakers, not superspies.

- ▶ **Use jargon sparingly.** Jargon is specialized or technical language that only makes sense to those in a specialized group, such as an industry or trade. Busy professionals also use jargon to explain a concept quickly. Not everyone in your audience will be familiar with the lingo of your industry. Try to select alternative terms that aren't overused.

- ▶ **Customize your words to your specific audience.** Know the work, focus, and concerns of your listeners. Tailor your vocabulary to accommodate the scope of their knowledge and cultural vernacular.

Observation #3: Inappropriate Language and References

- ▶ "The speaker's profanity (swearing and expletives) was off-putting."

- ▶ "Inappropriate language, jokes, and references."

160 PRESENTATION READY

Solutions

▶ **Refrain from using profanity.** Even if your intention is just to be funny or to swear simply for emphasis, it's not worth the risk of offending a listener or undermining your own credibility. Profanity is almost always considered a no-no unless you are a comedian doing stand-up. Good, clean, fun humor really can benefit your talk, and it is possible to get laughs without using profanity.

▶ **Find ways to foster inclusivity.** In a professional sales environment, you must be respectful and avoid any language that could be considered condescending, mocking, or racially and culturally insensitive. Refrain from using words that hold specific genders or communities of people up for ridicule or insult.

Observation #4: Verbal Clarity Issues

▶ "Not speaking clearly."

▶ "Mispronouncing words."

▶ "Using incorrect grammar."

Solutions

▶ **Be aware of how you sound.** Again, awareness is the key step in achieving verbal clarity. Be mindful of how you sound when you speak. Consider the successful speaker and business owner whose very polished British grandmother gently and consistently corrected her during childhood when she didn't enunciate clearly. When she spoke too quickly or ran her words together, her grandmother informed her that she sounded as if she had marbles in her mouth. Never a good thing. The bottom line? Speak in full sentences and use proper grammar in your conversations. Commit to doing the work. The more you practice, the more natural and eloquent you will sound over time.

- ▶ **Read aloud and practice tongue twisters.** Reading aloud for 15 minutes a day is a simple, straightforward strategy that can have a tremendous long-term impact on verbal clarity. For parents, reading aloud is a wonderful gift to give your children. Reading aloud can give them an opportunity to watch how other people phrase things, where to place emphasis, and how to use words properly. It's an engaging activity that helps improve diction and delivery.

  Diction relates to both your choice and use of words as well as to how clearly you pronounce them. Pronunciation is the way a person delivers the sounds of a word in speech.

An effective way to slow down and refine your speech is to recite tongue twisters. These unique verses remind us of the need to enunciate and force us to slow to a crawl. When you practice, be aware of the way your mouth, tongue, and lips move to produce the right sound to form the words. Here are few samples to try:

> Theophilus the thistle sifter
> While sifting a sifter full of thistles
> Thrust three thousand thistles
> Through the thick of his thumb.

> I stood on the steps of Burgesse's Fish Shop
> Mimicking him hiccupping
> And welcoming him in.

---

162 PRESENTATION READY

Silly Sally sits and shells her peas
All day long she sits and shells
And shells and sits
And sits and shells
And shells and sits.

Observation #5: Pitch, Intonation, Rate, and Volume Issues

▶ "Spoke with an odd cadence."

▶ "Had a flat, monotone voice and wore a blank expression."

▶ "Speaker's voice was so low it was difficult to hear well."

Solutions

▶ **Modulate pitch and intonation.** Anna Pasternak, a speech-
language pathologist with the College of Audiologists and
Speech-Language Pathologists of Ontario, explains it this way:
"Overall, the rise and fall in our voices allows for our speech
to be more interesting and dynamic as opposed to monotone."
Monotone makes it more difficult to read the emotion the person
is feeling and makes it more difficult to listen. When speaking
publicly, modulate your voice so that your overall tone is not
only pleasant but in step with the meaning of your words. First,
make sure your pitch—the highness and lowness of the tone of
your voice—is reasonably close to the middle. Second, keep your
intonation—the degree to which your pitch varies—nimble. Your
voice typically goes up in intonation when you are excited and
goes down in intonation when you are sad or confused. It's also
common to use a rise in intonation when you are emphasizing
specific words.

MISTAKE #12: VERBAL MISSTEPS 163

- **Control pace and rhythm.** Speak at a normal speed, taking calm, even breaths. You want to avoid rushing through so many words that you are gasping for breath at the end of a sentence. Don't be afraid to pause—for emphasis, effect, or mood, or to signal a transition to a new idea.

- **Use volume strategically.** Volume adds variety to whatever you are saying. Get louder or quieter when you want to emphasize a key point. In a one-on-one conversation, if someone is speaking softly to you, try to match the tone and volume. Conversely, if a prospect is loud and aggressive, you will want to be assertive yet still calm and pleasant, speaking in a quieter tone to avoid escalating the situation.

Observation #6: Personal Style Issues

- "Too argumentative."
- "Overly confident, cocky."
- "Too hungry or needy for the sale."
- "Too informal with the client."
- "A lack of confidence in presenting, selling."
- "The speaker insulted the prospects by flaunting their intelligence."
- "A noticeable lack of energy."
- "No enthusiasm for the topic."
- "Making active assumptions like, 'Let me tell you the truth!'"
- "Didn't seem natural, sounded like a script."
- "Too abrasive and direct, not likable."
- "Not speaking professionally."

164 PRESENTATION READY

Solutions

▶ **Speak in your authentic voice.** Your personal speaking style is the unique and genuine way you express yourself verbally. But many speakers repress their style and get stuck in the professional zone. They adopt a rigid posture, speak in a stilted voice, and remove all traces of personality from their message because they feel they're in professional mode. Oddly enough, when these same people are at a restaurant with friends a few hours later, talking about a crazy road trip or hilarious dating snafu, they're full of energy and laughter and completely different. The goal is to find a balance between those two personas, a style that integrates the professional and personal. When this misstep occurs, it's because a speaker has moved to one extreme or the other, failing to integrate the two approaches.

▶ **Apply emotional intelligence.** This issue taps into taking time to read the room. When speakers pair personal style with emotional intelligence—the ability to identify and manage one's own emotions as well as the emotions of others—they are better able to navigate a conversation or persuasive presentation. Emotional intelligence helps a speaker be fully present, listen actively to what audience members are saying, both verbally and nonverbally, and pivot toward or away from specific topics. When speakers fail to employ emotional intelligence, they can come off as too abrasive, too informal, or a little tone deaf.

▶ **Get clear on your personal style.** Take a time-out and ponder your personal style. How would you define it? How does it look and sound? As you review the personal style issues listed above, it's important to recognize that none of us want to be described as inauthentic or out of touch. No one enjoys being judged, but it happens all the time, and there's no avoiding it.

MISTAKE #12: VERBAL MISSTEPS **165**

Just as Eliza Doolittle was willing go through the awkwardness of elocution lessons and candid critiques of her speech, we must commit and do the often intricate and delicate work of becoming polished speakers. It might sound trite, but the most effective strategy to employ when dealing with verbal missteps is to show yourself a bit of grace as you are working through this. None of us are perfect. We are not robots. We are humans and we make mistakes. What's important is being able to recover quickly and elegantly when we do. It's about being as prepared as possible and nimble enough to right your boat when you hit rough water.

Summary

Mistake #12 is verbal missteps and relates to using language that is distracting, confusing, or inappropriate, calling a speaker's delivery skills into question.

- Speaking articulately and eloquently is a learned skill that must be developed and refined over time through study, awareness, and trial and error.
- Verbal missteps fall into six categories:
  1. Word redundancy and use of filler words
  2. Too much industry jargon or acronyms
  3. Inappropriate language or references
  4. Verbal clarity issues
  5. Rate, speed, and volume issues
  6. Personal style issues
- The most effective strategy when dealing with verbal missteps is to show yourself a bit of grace. We are human and we make mistakes. The key is being able to recover quickly and elegantly when we do.

▶ **Next Up.** Conclusion: Performance Tips and Conducting a Self-Evaluation

CONCLUSION

Performance Tips and Conducting a Self-Evaluation

In this Conclusion, you will take the final step in crafting a new and improved sales presentation. The goal is to apply the solutions discussed in this book, incorporating peer-to-peer learning and constructive feedback to make any final changes and adjustments you feel are necessary.

As discussed in the Introduction, you can't improve what you don't recognize as a problem. Recognition is the fastest way to course correct. In time, you will be able to transform your presentation almost overnight.

It's Go Time: Start with a Run-Through

Once you have crafted the first draft of your talk, it's imperative to do a run-through. Practice is essential preparation, and failure to practice is simply not in your best interest. Like a stage actor showing up at the theater for a dress rehearsal or a football team hitting the field for a scrimmage, it's time to deliver your presentation on camera. That means dressing up in the clothes you plan to wear during your presentation and executing a complete version for review. As Louis Pasteur said, "Chance favors the prepared mind."

For this practice run, you will need two things:

1. **A stopwatch.** You will want to measure how long it takes to deliver your talk. Some scenarios will afford you only a few minutes, while others will allow longer. Using a stopwatch will help you develop a sense of time and honor the time limits,

167

168 PRESENTATION READY

both real and implied, when you deliver your talk. (You most likely have a stopwatch at your fingertips on your smartphone or mobile device.)

2. **Presentation evaluation form.** The following form will guide you in analyzing your own presentation skills or those of your colleagues and associates to identify areas that need improvement.

Evaluating Your Performance

The presentation evaluation form is a simple, straightforward assessment tool that helps listeners critique a speaker's talk and determine whether it meets the key benchmarks we've outlined: case, creativity, and delivery.

Case
Did the speaker:

- ▶ Make the intention clear?
- ▶ Address the needs of the audience?
- ▶ Craft clean, logical arguments and key points?
- ▶ Use the bridge line, "What this means to you is . . ."?
- ▶ Cite sources and provide convincing evidence to support claims?
- ▶ Use a structured outline?
  - Introduction
  - Body
  - Conclusion
  - Close (Clear call to action)

Speech/Presentation Evaluation Form

PRESENTER'S NAME:

CASE	Excellent	Fine	Needs Work	CREATIVITY	Excellent	Fine	Needs Work	DELIVERY	Excellent	Fine	Needs Work

Did the speaker...

CASE				CREATIVITY				DELIVERY			
1. Make the intention clear?				1. Grab the listener's attention?				1. Display confidence and speak in an authentic voice?			
2. Address the needs of the audience?				2. Use engaging anecdotes, illustrations, and other support to create a compelling message?				2. Have good diction, word choice, and use of vocabulary?			
3. Craft clean, logical arguments and key points?				3. Use the allotted time in a balanced, effective manner?				3. Have energy and enthusiasm and/or engage the audience's attention with their presence?			
4. Use the bridge line, "What this means to you is . . ."?				4. Present thoughtful analysis of the content to the audience?				4. Use effective volume, rate, and pace when speaking?			
5. Cite sources and provide convincing evidence to support claims?				5. Use visual aids strategically?				5. Make any verbal missteps?			
6. Use a structured outline:				6. Tell timely stories that relate to the audience?				6. Dress appropriately?			
Introduction				7. Create a connection with listeners: ☐ In person ☐ Virtual ☐ Hybrid				7. Avoid distracting body language and engage in effective use of movement?			
Body								8. Manage any technology or demonstration issues?			
Conclusion								9. Show ability to manage external distractions?			
Close											

Notes:	EVALUATOR:
	TIME:

170 PRESENTATION READY

Creativity

Did the speaker:

- ▶ Grab the listener's attention?
- ▶ Use engaging anecdotes, illustrations, and other support to create a compelling message?
- ▶ Use the allotted time in a balanced, effective manner?
- ▶ Present thoughtful analysis of the content to the audience?
- ▶ Use visual aids strategically?
- ▶ Tell timely stories that relate to the audience?
- ▶ Create a connection with listeners:
  - In person
  - Virtual
  - Hybrid

Delivery

Did the speaker:

- ▶ Display confidence and speak in an authentic voice?
- ▶ Have good diction, word choice, and use of vocabulary?
- ▶ Have energy and enthusiasm and/or engage the audience's attention with their presence?
- ▶ Use effective volume, rate, and pace when speaking?
- ▶ Make any verbal missteps?
- ▶ Dress appropriately?
- ▶ Avoid distracting body language and engage in effective use of movement?

CONCLUSION: PERFORMANCE TIPS AND CONDUCTING A SELF-EVALUATION **171**

- ▶ Manage any technology or demonstration issues?
- ▶ Show ability to manage external distractions?

Options for Evaluating Your Presentation

It's helpful to remember that you have the option to record or not when staging your dress rehearsal. Consider the following options:

- ▶ **Develop a formal small-group evaluation session.** Bring together a small group of committed associates and create a space where everyone will participate in a positive and supportive environment. Take turns delivering your talks and sharing completed evaluation forms and feedback. Keep the atmosphere constructive and collegial.
- ▶ **Self-evaluate after giving a live, real-world talk.** Upon returning home from an actual presentation, take time to reflect and review your meeting using the form. Evaluate your message, noting what you think went well and what might need improvement.

Gracefully Accept Criticism

When you are criticized more than you care to be, don't let it distract you from your path or let someone else's feedback break you. Gracefully accept feedback, sifting through what is helpful and relevant to your situation and discarding what won't work for you. In the long run, the best feedback will help prevent you from giving suboptimal talks. As a result, you will become more confident, polished, persuasive, and consistent in delivering effective presentations.

Let's Talk About Feeling Nervous

The most effective dress rehearsals for this process are done on camera and in front of live listeners—a few trusted colleagues or close friends—who are willing to be candid about your presentation from the intended listeners' perspective. Sometimes, however, the mere thought of this exercise can send a person into a panic. Many speakers know their material well and understand how their presentation should be laid out, but when it comes to delivery—on camera or in person in front of their peers—their confidence wanes, so let's address a common problem for presenters—nervousness.

Nervousness exists on a continuum. We each have our own tolerance for stress, reacting differently to the same high-pressure situation. Some speakers feel mildly anxious before they speak in public and are referred to as *low communication-apprehensive* people. Others have a more extreme reaction, and they are known as *high communication-apprehensive* people. In severe cases of high communication-apprehension, a person might need to explore further whether sales is the best field to be in. Not everyone can grow accustomed to speaking in public, even one-on-one. If this is a great concern, consider reaching out to a specialized therapist in your community.

The signs of nervousness vary. The most common include a dry throat, moist palms, fluttery stomach, and even nausea, shortness of breath, and feet that feel like lead. Nervous feelings won't kill you, but they're certainly uncomfortable. These reactions are natural, physiological responses to placing yourself in a stressful situation. Some version of these symptoms is likely to stay with you if you continue to give presentations, because you care about the quality of your performance and the outcome.

As the saying goes, no pressure, no diamonds.

What's Behind Those Nervous Feelings?

There are various reasons speakers might feel nervous before a presentation. One of the most common is a lack of preparation, but it might also be due

CONCLUSION: PERFORMANCE TIPS AND CONDUCTING A SELF-EVALUATION **173**

to a general lack of self-confidence or a fear of failing. Even when all these issues are put to rest as well as humanly possible, nervousness might persist. As we scratch a little deeper beneath the surface for a reason, we realize how terribly exposed and vulnerable we feel in front of a major client or group. We know it is up to us to carry the weight of the entire dialogue.

Keep It to Yourself

Divulging your apprehension before a presentation doesn't typically help. Listeners won't know you are nervous if you don't let them in on the secret. If you must be open about it, tell them afterward. Telling listeners that you are nervous is not going to serve you. It might undermine your credibility. Some people see the opposite of being nervous as feeling confident and, therefore, capable.

It is common knowledge that before a competition we may experience the fear of failure as well as the desire for success. Giving a good sales presentation is competitive, so by its very nature it will cause some nervousness. Even the most seasoned competitors are nervous before an event. The better prepared you are, the less nervous you will be. The goal is to try public speaking, use tried-and-true techniques to ease your nerves, and monitor whether your anxiety starts diminishing. Most people adjust to the stress—but not everyone.

As you are coping with nerves and setting up to record your talk, pause long enough to take a deep breath, relax, and visualize yourself delivering a successful presentation. Imagine hitting it out of the park. Imagine the smile on your clients' faces when they have signed a contract or made a commitment to your project.

Polish Comes from Practice; Charisma Comes from Certainty

To achieve a successful outcome, you want to appear polished. Polished speakers have a smooth flow and a strong command of their material, audience, environment, and timing. The subtle quality of a true power speaker is charisma: the mesmerizing charm a person expresses in the presence of another. Charisma comes from self-confidence and the certainty of knowing what is happening and what is about to happen. Self-confidence emerges with control over thought, voice, and appearance. All these characteristics find their common root in individual practice.

> Self-knowledge is the beginning of self-improvement.
> —SPANISH PROVERB

Post-Evaluation Review

After completing your self-evaluation, revisit the mistakes we've discussed that pertain to the issues you want to course correct in your presentation. To set yourself up for success, you may also want to review this list of the 12 most common sales presentation mistakes and the action you can take to avoid each one.

Action Steps to Remedy the 12 Most Common Sales Presentation Mistakes

Case

- ▶ Mistake #1: "Winging it."
  Action Step: Define your goal or intention and examine your scenario, using the Presentation Opportunity General Information Form.

CONCLUSION: PERFORMANCE TIPS AND CONDUCTING A SELF-EVALUATION 175

▶ **Mistake #2: Being overly informative versus persuasive.**
Action Step: Identify your most compelling talking points to build your persuasive case.

▶ **Mistake #3: Providing inadequate support.**
Action Step: Use the Presentation Outline Worksheet to create the flow of your presentation, and determine where to incorporate evidence and support for your message.

▶ **Mistake #4: Failing to close the sale.**
Action Step: Identify your specific ask, Action Step, or close for this talk or meeting.

Creativity

▶ **Mistake #5: Misusing the allotted time.**
Action Step: Calculate how to balance your time and content effectively. "Do the math."

▶ **Mistake #6: Being boring, boring, boring.**
Action Step: Review your outline and incorporate creativity to bring your message to life.

▶ **Mistake #7: Ineffectively using visual aids.**
Action Step: Strategize on how to best use visual aids to emphasize key points.

▶ **Mistake #8: Failure to create connection with listeners.**
Action Step: Employ pathos, logos, ethos to create connection with listeners.

Delivery

▶ **Mistake #9: Distracting gestures and body language.**
Action Step: Video record your presentation to stay aware of your physical presence and gesturing.

176 PRESENTATION READY

- ▶ **Mistake #10: Dressing inappropriately or unprofessionally.**
  Action Step: Determine how to best dress for the environment and the opportunity you are seeking.

- ▶ **Mistake #11: Technology or demonstration failures.**
  Action Step: Review your Simple Video & Tech-Ready Checklist and do a pre-presentation run-through.

- ▶ **Mistake #12: Verbal missteps.**
  Action Step: Practice your presentation with an awareness of your verbal clarity and delivery.

These 12 mistakes are common, are easy to make, and can negatively impact a speaker's overall success. They also have clear solutions that you can use in the planning stages to create clear, compelling, and effective messages or to recover gracefully in the moment.

Conclusion

Whether your next presentation is 3 minutes or 30 minutes, that's not a lot of time, and brevity is your friend. No one has ever said, "Gosh, I wish that sales presentation had been longer." Ultimately, it's not about the specific time allotted but rather making the most of the time you have.

You are one person with an authentic, compelling message, standing before a receptive listener, and you have the power to shift everything. But you must use it. Don't fail to launch or second-guess your talk's value because you are preoccupied with achieving perfection. As we noted in the Preface, neither presentations nor the speakers who deliver them are perfect. Everyone has good days and bad days. The good news is that a presentation doesn't have to be perfect to work. All you need to do is give it your best effort, practice consistently, and try to have more on days than off days.

The intention of this book is to help you view your future presentations through a different lens. By learning on your own and from others, you can grow and have more consistent, positive outcomes that lead to amazing opportunities. On this path, you will craft presentations that work well and others that don't. Some might work for a while and then not again. You might land the deal you want on the first try, or you might not succeed until several attempts later. You will win and lose along the way, and that's all okay. Enjoy the ride.

Trust in yourself and your ability. You can do this. Give yourself a chance. Give your dream a chance. Use your voice for good.

And with that—congratulations! You are Presentation Ready.

APPENDIX A

Research and Methodology

State of Sales Presentations Research Summary

This national study builds on our previous work around sales presentations and has been released in three phases. The goal is to further examine the art and science of delivering an effective presentation to move a transaction forward.

Phase One

The first phase of this study, released on March 4, 2020, examined the habits of more than 2,500 sales professionals whose livelihoods depended on their ability to build and deliver persuasive presentations. This research helped clarify the different types of presentation mistakes made and their relevance in today's professional sales environment. Quantitative survey items measured the prevalence of making and observing the original 9 sales presentation mistakes published in the book *New Sales Speak* (Wiley, 2001). Qualitative survey items asked participants to describe additional mistakes they made or observed, which they perceived as impacting sales success. A qualitative thematic analysis of these responses identified 3 additional presentation mistakes in today's competitive sales environment. The findings provide empirical support for 12 common presentation mistakes professionals make and their implications for buyers and sellers. The data gathered reflects an entirely pre-pandemic work environment.

Phase Two

Shortly after the release of the Phase One report, due to the impact of the coronavirus pandemic, we observed that video platforms were emerging as the dominant presentation tool and deserved exploration. We designed a second phase of the study to gain a greater understanding of the impact of the most common presentation mistakes made within a predominantly virtual work environment. For almost two years, Sjodin Communications held persuasive presentation skills workshops and seminars, collecting data from 1,038 sales professionals presenting remotely via a videoconferencing platform. The results report, released August 19, 2022, also made comparisons between Phase One and Phase Two findings.

Phase Three

Phase Three of the research was a crucial continuation of the preceding two phases. This phase investigated the 12 sales presentation mistakes most often committed by sales professionals and the efficacy of sales presentations across in-person, videoconference, and hybrid environments. A total of 1,075 individuals completed the Phase Three survey. The results report was released September 18, 2023.

In this phase of the study, we defined videoconferencing as meetings made possible by online technology that lets users in multiple locations hold face-to-face meetings without having to occupy the same physical space. A hybrid meeting involves a mixture of in-person and remote attendees. Remote attendees join the meeting via a virtual meeting platform, such as Microsoft Teams or Zoom. In-person attendees sit together in a dedicated meeting room.

Participants, Narrow Focus, and Transparency

This research exclusively targeted business development professionals whose livelihoods depend on their ability to build and deliver persuasive presentations, whether they promote a product, service, or cause. The entirety of the data collected was self-reported by business and sales professionals, examining their perspectives on mistakes made while delivering and observing sales presentations. We shared the survey results with the organization hosting the event and held a post-event Q&A/review to discuss the findings, including the nuances of the current selling presentation environment.

Timing

The sales presentation landscape has changed. The timing of this study is unique because it analyzed changes in the reported experiences of sales professionals over time—from 2018 to 2023—specifically the incorporation of in-person, virtual, and hybrid presentations into the sales process.

Leadership and Participant Reflections

This report used reflections, a qualitative tool that allowed researchers to share results with participants and provide a space to discuss themes and issues emerging from the analysis. This process, combined with data observations, generated multiple discussion points and actionable solution steps.

Methodology

The three phases used a mixed methodology to examine the extent to which sales professionals commit the 12 presentation mistakes, whether in person, virtual, or hybrid. A survey was designed and implemented using Qualtrics and Survey Monkey. Participants were recruited using nonrandom convenience sampling through workshops and seminars for organizations hosting Sjodin Communications programs. When the company administrators were willing to share the link with their employees via email, the link was sent before, during, and/or after the Sjodin

182 APPENDIX A: RESEARCH AND METHODOLOGY

Communications lecture. Otherwise, the survey link was made available to audiences via QR codes and Bitly links at the lecture's conclusion.

A post-event call was conducted with Sjodin Communications and the organization's leaders that sponsored the event. Organizational leaders received and reviewed a detailed summary report of the survey findings, followed by an open-ended discussion to explore member reflections on the report. The results from these discussions clarified the data collected and offered unique insights into specific themes discussed above.

The data reflects the self-reported responses of participants. Given the large, nonrandom sample, statistical interpretations required the confidence level for determined significance to be 99 percent confident to infer a meaningful relationship. All findings reflect that level of confidence.

To review the summary reports, please visit https://www.sjodin communications.com/state-of-sales-presentations-research-study-reports.

APPENDIX B

Forms

What follows is a copy of each of the user forms referred to throughout the book.

FORM #1   Presentation Opportunity General Information Form Blank (Chapter 1)

FORM #2   Presentation Outline Worksheet Form Blank (Chapter 5)

FORM #3   Blank Short Outline Form (4 x 6 Card) (Chapter 5)

FORM #4   Six-Point Star Diagram (Chapter 9)

FORM #5   Simple Video & Tech-Ready Checklist (Chapter 11)

FORM #6   Speech/Presentation Evaluation Form Blank (Conclusion)

In addition to the blank forms in this Appendix, you can access a larger version of each document at www.sjodincommunications.com.

Presentation Ready

PRESENTATION OPPORTUNITY
GENERAL INFORMATION FORM

I. WHAT IS THE GOAL (OR INTENTION) OF YOUR PRESENTATION?

....

....

II. AUDIENCE ANALYSIS INFORMATION

- Who are the listeners? ....
- Audience size? ....
- Average age of group? ....
- Gender ratio? ....
- Attitude of audience? ....
- How informed is the audience? ....

III. LOGISTICAL INFORMATION

- In person, virtual, or hybrid ....
- Visual aid options ....
- Time allotted for presentation ....
- Who speaks before/after you ....

IV. WHAT IS THE BEST WAY TO CLOSE IN THIS SITUATION?

....

....

APPENDIX B: FORMS **185**

Presentation Ready

PRESENTATION OUTLINE WORKSHEET

I. INTRODUCTION: **(Attention Step)**
- Grab the listener's attention: (Establish a friendly feeling and arouse audience curiosity.)

  ....

- Tell the listener where you are going:

  ....

II. BODY
1. Talking Point #1 *(Ex. Why Me?)*
   a. Argument: **(Need Step)** ....

   b. Proof and/or illustration: **(Satisfaction Step)** ....

   ....
   c. So what? What this means to you is . . . **(Visualization Step)**

   ....

2. Talking Point #2 *(Ex. Why My Organization/Company?)*
   a. Argument: **(Need Step)** ....

   b. Proof and/or illustration: **(Satisfaction Step)** ....

   ....
   c. So what? What this means to you is . . . **(Visualization Step)**

   ....

3. Talking Point #3 *(Ex. Why Now?)*
   a. Argument: **(Need Step)** ....

   b. Proof and/or illustration: **(Satisfaction Step)** ....

   ....
   c. So what? What this means to you is . . . **(Visualization Step)**

   ....

III. CONCLUSION: WRAP UP (Transition into Action Step)
- Reiterate the three points **(Conclude the Visualization Step)**

  ....

- **Optional:** Suggest a couple of intriguing topics that you can discuss with the listener in your next appointment. (Give the person a reason to want to hear more.)

  ....

IV. CLOSE: CALL TO ACTION **(Action Step)**
- Make your offer of service. State what you want to happen as a result of your presentation. (For example: "It is my goal to learn more about your needs and how I might be of service to your company...") This serves as a soft transition to your close.

  ....

- Ask for the next appointment time, referral, lead, introduction, opportunity, or whatever will help you initiate the next step in the process.

  ....

BLANK SHORT OUTLINE FORM (4X6 CARD)

I. INTRODUCTION
- Grab the listener's attention...
- Tell them where you are going...

II. BODY
- Talking point #1...
- Talking point #2...
- Talking point #3...

III. CONCLUSION
- Wrap up. (Allude to a couple of strong points you
  wish to discuss in detail if given additional time.)

....

IV. CLOSE: CALL TO ACTION
- Ask for an appointment time to give them a longer, more in-depth presentation.

....

APPENDIX B: FORMS 187

Presentation Ready

SIX POINT STAR DIAGRAM
Moving with Transitions

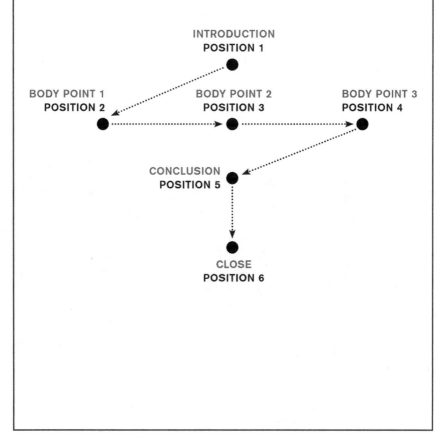

Simple Video & Tech Ready Checklist

Set the Stage

☐ Location – Where is the best space for your setup?
☐ Ambience – What mood are you trying to convey?
☐ Background – Does your background encourage connection with the audience?

Lighting

☐ Soft, diffused lighting is best, should be behind the camera, and shining on your face.
☐ Watch for dim lighting, harsh shadows, and bright light shining through open blinds.
☐ Invest in a LED light, or small desk lamp with diffusion to create soft light.

Your In-Person and/or On-Screen Image

☐ Look your best—makeup, hair, and clothes. It's showtime!
☐ If you're going on camera, set the camera just above eye level and tilt slightly downward. (Stack your laptop or tablet on books or boxes to achieve the height you need.)
☐ Make virtual eye contact by looking directly into the camera, not at yourself on the screen.
☐ Center your head and torso and take up most of the frame.
☐ Remember you are the star. Don't let your visual aids overshadow your message.

Sound

☐ Speak clearly and make sure that it's easy to hear you.
☐ Upgrade to a high-quality microphone to get better overall sound.
☐ Conduct a microphone check with a friend or colleague to get feedback on your vocal tone and clarity.
☐ Control background noise, particularly when working from home.
☐ Consider using noise-blocking apps.

Gear

☐ Determine if your computer is prepared for optimum delivery.
☐ Use Wi-Fi, wired/hardline, or both.
☐ Use a high-quality webcam to improve visual image, warmth, resolution, and depth of picture.
☐ Make sure bandwidth and network latency are at optimum capabilities for your needs. (Bandwidth is measured as the amount of data that can be transferred from one point to another within a network in a specific amount of time. Network latency is the amount of time it takes for data or a request to go from the source to its destination. It is measured in milliseconds, and the closer your latency is to zero, the better.)

Plan B

☐ In case of system failure, what is your backup plan?

Speech/Presentation Evaluation Form

PRESENTER'S NAME:

CASE	Excellent	Fine	Needs Work	CREATIVITY	Excellent	Fine	Needs Work	DELIVERY	Excellent	Fine	Needs Work

Did the speaker...

CASE				CREATIVITY				DELIVERY			
1. Make the intention clear?				1. Grab the listener's attention?				1. Display confidence and speak in an authentic voice?			
2. Address the needs of the audience?				2. Use engaging anecdotes, illustrations, and other support to create a compelling message?				2. Have good diction, word choice, and use of vocabulary?			
3. Craft clean, logical arguments and key points?				3. Use the allotted time in a balanced, effective manner?				3. Have energy and enthusiasm and/or engage the audience's attention with their presence?			
4. Use the bridge line, "What this means to you is..."?				4. Present thoughtful analysis of the content to the audience?				4. Use effective volume, rate, and pace when speaking?			
5. Cite sources and provide convincing evidence to support claims?				5. Use visual aids strategically?				5. Make any verbal missteps?			
6. Use a structured outline:				6. Tell timely stories that relate to the audience?				6. Dress appropriately?			
Introduction				7. Create a connection with listeners: ☐ In person ☐ Virtual ☐ Hybrid				7. Avoid distracting body language and engage in effective use of movement?			
Body								8. Manage any technology or demonstration issues?			
Conclusion								9. Show ability to manage external distractions?			
Close											

Notes:	EVALUATOR:
	TIME:

Acknowledgments

The gift of the acknowledgments section is that it's an author's chance to formally thank the people who have supported the writing of her book, and give the readers a bit of understanding that no one accomplishes a goal like writing, releasing, and selling a book without the help of numerous people. The credit for this book is shared with many dear friends and associates.

This project is the culmination of my work over the course of my career. What an incredible adventure!

With sincere gratitude, I would like to thank my team, family, friends, and colleagues who have helped bring this idea into form.

My personal editor, Kari Barlow, has been a trusted friend and indispensable colleague in bringing this book to life. She has worked with me through the years to help convert my writing, speeches, lectures, and seminar content into a manuscript that reflects the core of my life's work—this has been no easy feat! I am thankful for her ability to help me finesse the words I share with the world in written form.

Christopher Ferebee, my literary agent, has believed in me and this project from the beginning—we did it! Thank you!

Thanks to the team at McGraw Hill, and editor Michele Matrisciani, for believing in this book.

I am particularly grateful for the SDSU team that supported my State of Sales Presentations research study: Dr. Heather E. Canary, Dr. Rachael A. Record, and Giuliano I. McDonald. Their insight, analysis, and perspective have been the baseline for this project.

The women on the Sjodin Communications Administrative Marketing and Support Team—Jennie Ritchie, Madison Potts, and

Katelyn Lucas—have been an integral part of developing, organizing, and managing this content. Your loyalty and support over the years have been a notable part of the evolution of this work.

I would also like to express my deep appreciation to the many corporations, associations, and individuals who participated in the various phases of the State of Sales Presentations research study.

A special thank you goes out to my dear friend and mentor Harvey Mackay. Your advice has been invaluable to me over the years.

A big thank you to David Amaral, owner of Phantom Design, for his creative contributions to this work and for his friendship and unwavering support.

Thank you to Mitt Seely for his inventive illustrations in this book.

Thank you to Mark Fortier with Fortier Public Relations for his commitment to this project before, during, and after the launch.

A very special thank you goes out to my colleagues and friends at The Mackay Roundtable, National Speakers Association, and Gen Next/Alder Crew.

My parents, Jan and Pete Sjodin, my sister Kim Sjodin-Caminiti, and my extended family members were all part of the manuscript review team or helped promote the book. I love you guys.

Friends are the family we choose. My dearest friends, old and new, are all such a wonderful gift. On this particular project, I want to give a shout-out to James Corboy, Courtney Noelle Maddox, Joey Walker-Bialek, Monique Egan, Nick Taylor, Nicole Najoan, Pattie Scoma, and Tiffany Ashland-Lemos for their time and consistent willingness to let me share the ups and downs on this roller coaster ride!

Thank you all for being part of my journey.

Bibliography

Aristotle. *Rhetoric*. Mineola, NY: Dover Publications, 2004.

"Barack Obama's New Hampshire Primary Speech." *New York Times*, January 8, 2008, https://www.nytimes.com/2008/01/08/us/politics/08text-obama.html.

Calhoun, Lisa. "Science Reveals the Right Timing for Eye Contact." *Inc.* magazine, July 7, 2016, https://www.inc.com/lisa-calhoun/how-long-you -should-make-eye-contact-according-to-science.html.

Dress for Success. "About Us." Accessed January 5, 2023, https://dressforsucces s.org/about-us/.

"5 Reasons to Use Visual Aids for Speeches and Presentations." Microsoft, July 7, 2021, https://www.microsoft.com/en-us/microsoft-365-life-hacks/ presentations/five-reasons-to-use-visual-aids-for-speeches-and-presentations.

Ehninger, Douglas, Bruce E. Gronbeck, Ray E. McKerrow, and Alan H. Monroe. *Principles and Types of Speech Communication*, 10th ed. Glenview, IL: Scott Foresman, 1986.

Gallo, Carmine. "The Art of Persuasion Hasn't Changed in 2,000 Years." *Harvard Business Review*, July 15, 2019, https://hbr.org/2019/07/the-art-of -persuasion-hasnt-changed-in-2000-years.

Gallo, Carmine. *The Presentation Secrets of Steve Jobs: How to Be Insanely Great in Front of Any Audience*. New York: McGraw Hill, 2009.

Goldin-Meadow, Susan. "Amanda Gorman, Poet Laureate and Gesture Laureate." *Scientific American*, March 8, 2021, https://www.scientificamerican .com/article/amanda-gorman-poet-laureate-and-gesturer-laureate/.

Horsager, Dave. *Trusted Leader: 8 Pillars That Drive Results*. Oakland, CA: Berrett-Koehler, 2021.

King, Larry. "Special Tribute to Paul Harvey." *CNN Larry King Live*, https:// transcripts.cnn.com/show/lkl/date/2009-03-01/segment/01.

194 BIBLIOGRAPHY

Kouzes, James M., and Barry Z. Posner. *Credibility: How Leaders Gain and Lose It, Why People Demand It*. San Francisco: Jossey-Bass, 2011.

Lambert, Fred. "Elon Musk: Tesla Cybertruck Glass Demo Fail Helped Electric Truck Get Attention." Electrek, April 26, 2020, https://electrek.co/2020/04/26/tesla-cybertruck-glass-demo-fail-elon-musk-electric-truck-attention/.

Leeds, Dorothy. *PowerSpeak*. New York: Berkeley Publishing Group, 1991.

My Fair Lady. Lyrics by Alan Jay Lerner. Music by Frederick Loewe. Mark Hellinger Theatre, New York, March 15, 1956.

New Yorker cartoon by Alex Gregory, "Death by PowerPoint." First published in the *New Yorker* in 2003. Licensing rights are through CartoonStock.

Oh, D., E. Shafir, and A. Todorov. "Economic Status Cues from Clothes Affect Perceived Competence from Faces." *Nature Human Behaviour* 4 (2020): 287–293.

Pasternak, Anna. "Differences Between Pitch, Intonation, and Inflection." Well Said, Toronto Speech Therapy, February 10, 2021, https://www.torontospeechtherapy.com/blog/2021/pitch-intonation-and-inflection.

Petry, Andrew C. "Communication Apprehension Affects Performance." Master's thesis, John Carroll University, 2016, pp. 1–51, https://collected.jcu.edu/cgi/viewcontent.cgi?article=1048&context=mastersessays.

Seinfeld. Season 5, Episode 18, "The Raincoats." Directed by Tom Cherones. Aired April 28, 1994, on CBS.

Shaw, George Bernard. *Pygmalion*. Mineola, NY: Dover Publications, 1994.

Shu, Suzanne B., and Kurt A. Carlson. "When Three Charms but Four Alarms: Identifying the Optimal Number of Claims in Persuasion Settings." *Journal of Marketing* 78, no. 1 (2014): 127–139, https://doi.org/10.1509/jm.11.0504.

Sjodin, Terri. *New Sales Speak: The 9 Biggest Sales Presentation Mistakes & How to Avoid Them*. New York: Wiley, 2006.

Sjodin, Terri. *Small Message, Big Impact*. New York: Penguin Portfolio, 2011.

Sjodin, Terri. *State of Sales Presentations Research Study Results Phase One*. Newport Beach, CA: Sjodin Communications, 2021.

Sjodin, Terri. *State of Sales Presentations Research Study Results Phase Two*. Newport Beach, CA: Sjodin Communications, 2022.

Sjodin, Terri. *State of Sales Presentations Research Study Results Phase Three*. Newport Beach, CA: Sjodin Communications, 2023.

Speed, Richard. "Twenty Years Ago Today: Windows 98 Crashed Live on Stage with Bill Gates. Let's Watch It Again . . . ." The Register, April 20, 2018, https://www.theregister.com/2018/04/20/windows_98_comdex_bsod_video/.

Streisand, Barbra, director. *The Mirror Has Two Faces*. Burbank, CA: TriStar Pictures, 1996.

Truman, Harry. "September 18, 1948: Whistlestop Tour in Chariton, Iowa." Transcript, https://millercenter.org/the-presidency/presidential-speeches/september-18-1948-whistlestop-tour-chariton-iowa.

Waldman, Michael. *My Fellow Americans: The Most Important Speeches of American Presidents, from George Washington to George W. Bush*. Norwalk, CT: Easton Press, 2003.

"Zoom Statistics 2022: How Video Conferencing Changed Our Lives." TeamStage, accessed February 1, 2023, https://teamstage.io/zoom-statistics/#general-zoom-and-video-conferencing-statistics.

Index

Accents, style and, 156
Acronyms, 157–159
Action, 20
    calls to, 41, 46–47, 49, 61
    connection and, 100, 113
    impact and, 26
    outlines and, 57
Action Step, of Motivated Sequence,
    23, 42–44, 49, 58, 106
Action steps, 44, 174–176
    goals and, 43
Adaptation
    to audience, 106–107
    time and, 55
    understanding and, 100
Alliteration, 77
Amaral, David, 142
Analogy, 76
Analysis, 108
    of data, 35–36, 179
    evidence and, 31–32
    of skills, 168
Anaphora, 77
Anchor words, 60
Anecdotes, 76, 78
Answers, 25
    preparation of, 10, 13
Antithesis, 77
Anxiety, body language and, 121–122,
    173. *See also* Nervousness

Aposiopesis, 78
Appeal, 61, 103, 111–112
    visual, 87–88
Appointments, close of sale and,
    43–46, 61
Arguments, 11, 13
    clarity and, 21–24
    close of sale and, 29
    creativity and, 78, 82
    evidence and, 23, 31–32, 76
    with impact, 26–28
    outcomes and, 21
    specificity and, 24–26
Aristotle, *Rhetoric*, 101–102, 104,
    110, 112
Armstrong, Neil, 77
Ask, 29, 46, 49
    specificity of, 43–44
Assessment, 168–170
    of self, 158, 171
Assumptions, 163
    questions and, 106
Attention, of audience, 60, 80,
    123
    connection and, 75–76
    lighting and, 150
    nonverbals and, 118–119
    visual aids and, 86
Attention Step, of Motivated
    Sequence, 22, 58

198 INDEX

Audience, xiii, 8, 36. *See also*
Attention, of audience; Remote
audiences
adaptation to, 106–107
connection with, 75–76, 80–82,
99–102
content and, 81
culture of, 131–133, 137, 158–159
interest and, 73, 80
listening to, 106–107
memory of, 61, 70, 86
needs of, 51
questions of, 23, 25
specificity and, 38
time constraints and, 53–54
understanding of, 33, 74
visual aids and, 87, 90–94, 98
Authenticity, 164, 170, 174
connection and, 103, 105–107,
113
of message, 103–104
Avoidance, of close, 41, 43
Awareness, 167
clarity and, 160–161
of nonverbals, 120–122
verbal skills and, 156–157

Backup plans, 144, 152
outlines as, 146–147, 153
for visual aids, 96
Balance, 17, 38–39
of content, 53
creativity and, 78
data and, 28–29, 32
in message, 35–36
of talking points, 56
time and, 71, 73
visual aids and, 87–88
Bandwidth, failure of, 140, 144

Belief, 13, 34, 103, 105
Bias, 19–20, 107
Biden, Joe, 127
"Boat test," 99–100
Body, of presentations, 58, 60–61, 86,
124
Body language, 117–118, 125–126
anxiety and, 121–122, 173
focus and, 123
hybrid presentations and,
119–120
meanings and, 127–128
reflections on, 119–120, 122–124
Boring presentations, xviii, 77–79
informative compared to, 73–74
reflections on, 74–76, 80–82
Brainstorm, 79
Brevity, 176
specificity and, 28
Bullet point lists, as visual aids,
90–94

Calls, to action, 41, 46–47, 49, 61
Carlson, Kurt A., 60–61
Case, xx, 1, 168
action steps for, 174–175
close of sale and, 41–49
improvisation and, 3–15
information overload and, 17–29
support for, 31–40
Case Arguments, 26–27
Categories, of presentations, 19–20
Ceremonial presentations, 20
Certainty, 40, 133, 152
charisma and, 174
Challenges, 122
backup plans and, 147
nervousness and, 151
opportunities and, 64

INDEX 199

Charisma, certainty and, 174
Checklist, for technology, 142–145, 153
Churchill, Winston, 7
Clarity, xxi, 11, 27, 43–44
  in arguments, 21–24
  data dumps and, 20–21
  intention and, 12–13
  persuasion and, 18–19
  style and, 164
  time and, 54–57, 70
  verbal, 157, 160–162
  visual aids and, 88, 92
Close, of sale, xviii, 44, 58
  arguments and, 29
  avoidance of, 41, 43
  body language and, 124
  call to action and, 61
  conclusion and, 41–43, 49
  data dumps and, 28
  hard sells and, 43, 46–47
  information overload and, 27–28
  opportunity and, 47–48
  persuasion and, 42, 46
  presentation formats and, 45, 54
  reflections on, 42–43, 45
  time allotment and, 62
Close talk, 119, 126
Clothing. *See* Dress
Colleagues, practice and, 9–12, 120, 144, 168, 172–173
Color, of dress, 137
Commitment, 34, 42
  pivot strategy and, 45–46
Competence, 129, 141, 155
Competition, xiii–xv, 17, 36, 39, 108–109, 173
  cooperation and, 19–20
  interviews with, 79

Components, of presentation, 56, 58–61, 66–69, 71
Comprehensive listening, 108
Conclusion, of presentations, 58, 61, 63
  body language and, 124
  close of sale and, 41–43, 49
Confidence, xvi, 13, 172–173, 182
  credibility and, 109
  dress and, 131, 133–135, 137–138
  overconfidence and, 3, 108–109, 163
  verbal skills and, 156
Connection, xix, 108–109, 111–112, 175
  action and, 100, 113
  with audience, 75–76, 80–82, 99–102
  authenticity and, 103, 105–107, 113
  dress and, 130
  humor and, 104
  nonverbals and, 126
  persuasion and, 100–101, 148
  visual aids and, 110
Constraints. *See* Time constraints
Content, 13, 15
  audience and, 81
  balance of, 53
  customized, xx, 26, 60, 75, 106–107, 158–159
  nonverbals and, 117
  time and, 56–57
Conversation, 7, 10
  outlines and, 57, 64
  visual aids and, 87, 90
Conversions, xix, 17–18, 27
Cooperation, competition and, 19–20
Coronavirus pandemic, x, 4, 179–180
  pivots and, 93–96

200 INDEX

Craft, of message, 1, 19–22, 24, 80, 167–168
Creativity, xx, 51, 152, 170
  action steps for, 175
  boring presentations and, 73–83
  connection and, 99–113
  graphic design and, 110–112
  mindset of, 79–80
  time allotment and, 53–71
  visual aids and, 85–98
Credibility, 32–33, 36, 40
  attention and, 76
  confidence and, 109
  dress and, 129, 138
  ethos and, 102–103
  message and, 34
  nervousness and, 173
  statistics and, 37
  verbal skills and, 155–156
Credibility (Kouses and Pozner), 34
Critical listening, 108
Critique, 168
  grace and, 171
  of verbal skills, 165
Culture, of audience, 131–133, 137
  jargon and, 158–159
Curiosity, 22, 51, 80, 88
Customized content, xx, 26, 60, 75, 106–107. *See also* Tailored presentations
  language and, 51
  verbal skills and, 158–159

Data, x–xi, xvi, 33–34, 76, 82
  analysis of, 35–36, 179
  balance and, 28–29, 32
  connection and, 108
  on dress, 129–130
  logos and, 102

  storytelling and, 75, 104
  as support, 37
Data dumps, 17–19
  balance and, 32
  clarity and, 20–21
  close of sale and, 28
Decisions, 28
  follow-up and, 45–46
  information overload and, 18, 24
  support and, 31
Delivery, xx, 115, 170–171
  acronyms and, 157–159
  action steps for, 175
  body language and, 117–128
  demonstration failures and, 139–153
  dress and, 129–138
  facial expressions and, 121
  human error and, 139–141, 148–153
  pauses in, 158, 163, 173
  skills of, 155, 166
  stiff, 9, 119, 126, 164
  verbal mistakes and, 155–166
  volume of, 162–163
Demonstration failures, 139, 143–145, 148–150
  pivots and, 151–152
  presentation formats and, 140–141
  reflections on, 142, 146–147
Demonstrations, 87, 89
  as support, 38
Design
  graphic, 110–112
  of visual aids, 92, 111
Diction, 158, 161–162, 170
Distraction, 149, 171
  improvisation and, 4, 12

language and, 155, 166
nonverbals and, 117, 119–120, 123,
    125–126, 128
Diversity, connection and, 112
Dress
    confidence and, 131, 133–135,
        137–138
    credibility and, 129, 138
    data on, 129–130
    inappropriate, 129–132, 137–138
    message and, 129, 137–138
    reflections on, 131–133
    style and, 132, 136
    unprofessional, 129–130, 138
    videoconference presentations
        and, 130–132
Dress codes, 130
Dress for Success, 134–135

Ease of use argument, 27
Effectiveness, time and, 54, 62–70
Effort, xx, 12, 109, 115, 137, 176
Emotion, pathos and, 102–103
Emotional intelligence, 164
Empathetic listening, 107–108
Energy
    of audience, 98
    nonverbals and, 124–128
    of presenter, 12, 73, 80–82
Engagement, visual aids and, 86–87,
    94–96
Enhancement, visual aids and, 86, 88,
    92, 96
Entertainment, 75
    speech supports and, 80
Error
    human, 139–141, 148–153
    trial and, xiv, 155, 166
Ethics, in sales, 33–34

Ethos, connection and, 101–104,
    109–113, 175
Evaluation, 34, 96, 168–171, 174.
    See also Critique
Evidence, 1, 37, 70
    arguments and, 23, 31–32, 76
    speech supports and, 78, 82
    storytelling and, 32, 35–36, 39, 40
Execution, xx, 115, 139, 151, 155
Experience
    immersive, 89, 151
    lack of, 33–34
    sensory, 86, 88
    visual, 38
Explanation, 17, 42
    connection and, 100–101
Extemporaneous format, 8–9
Eye contact, 119, 128
    intention and, 122
    remote audiences and, 149
    virtual, 143

Facial expressions, 121
Failure, 100, 176. *See also*
    Demonstration failures;
    Technology failures
    of bandwidth, 140, 144
    fear of, 172–173
Fear, 119
    of failure, 172–173
    of rejection, 41, 49
Feedback, practice and, 167–171, 174
Filler words, 155, 157–158, 166
Flipcharts, 89
Flow, 5, 12, 146, 151, 174, 175
Focus
    body language and, 123
    improvisation and, 12–13
    technology failure and, 150–151

202 INDEX

Follow-up, 45–46, 62, 140
Formats, speech, 7–11
Forms
    Presentation Opportunity General
        Information, 5–6, 12, 63–65,
        71, 174
    Short Outline, 64, 69
Frame of mind, 4, 12
Franklin, Benjamin, 75
Friendliness, 100, 103, 109, 121
Fun argument, 27
Function, style and, 129

Gallo, Carmine, 104
Gates, Bill, 146
General presentations, 26–27, 64–65,
    71
Gestures, 118, 120, 121, 125–126
Goals, xvii–xviii, 3, 49, 61
    action steps and, 43
    listening and, 107
Gorman, Amanda, 127
Grace, 55, 127, 133, 165–166, 171,
    176
Graphic design, 110–112

Handouts, 8, 11, 89
Hard sells, 20–21
    close of sale and, 43, 46–47
Harvey, Paul, 134
Henry, Patrick, 99–100
High-tech visual aids, 88–90, 96
Home offices, 132
Home studios, 95–96
Horsager, Dave, *Trusted Leader*,
    110
Human error, 139–141, 152–153
    preparation and, 150
    reflections on, 148–151

Humor, 125–126
    connection and, 104
    pain points and, 93–94
    stories and, 81
Hybrid presentations, xix, 148–149,
    153, 180–181
    body language and, 119–120

Immersive experiences, 89, 151
Impact
    arguments with, 26–28
    of dress, 138
    of message, 57
Impressions, 37, 103, 129–130, 133
Impromptu format, 7–8
Improvement, xii, xiv, 155
    practice and, 151, 171
    quantified, 31
Improvisation, 6–10, 14
    backup plans and, 147
    distraction and, 4, 12
    focus and, 12–13
    preparation and, 3, 11, 15
    reflections on, 4–5, 11–12
Inadequate support, 31–33
Inappropriate dress, 129–132,
    137–138
Inappropriate language, 155, 157,
    159–160, 166
Inclusivity, 160
Informal style, 131, 163–164
Information, 36, 56, 70, 108
    action steps and, 44
    irrelevant, 33
Information overload, 22–23, 25–26,
    29
    close of sale and, 27–28
    decisions and, 18, 24
    hard sells and, 20–21

INDEX 203

persuasion compared to, xviii,
17–18, 20, 28
reflections on, 18–21
Informative presentations, 19–20
boring compared to, 73–74
In-person presentations, xix, 4, 45,
180–181
creativity and, 75–76
time constraints and, 53–55
Intelligence, emotional, 164
Intention, 12–14, 20, 107, 122–123
Interaction, 7, 89, 148–149
Interest
audience and, 73, 80
in message, 82–83
Interviews
with competition, 79
job, 44, 47–48
Intonation, 162–163
Introduction, of presentations, 56, 58,
60–61
body language and, 124
Investment, 44, 135
return on, 36
Irrelevant information, 33

Jargon, 155, 157, 166
audience culture and, 158–159
Job interviews, 44, 47–48
Jobs, Steve, 136
Judgments, 34, 108, 129

Kouzes, James M., *Credibility*, 34

Lack, of experience, 33–34
Language. *See also* Body language
customized, 51
distraction and, 155, 166
inappropriate, 155, 157, 159–160, 166

Laughter, 75, 78–79. *See also* Humor
Less, as More, 63, 92
Lighting
attention and, 150
in virtual presentations, 143, 149
Likeability, 163
"boat test" and, 99–100
trust and, 109–110
Listeners. *See* Audience
Listening, 74, 100
to audience, 106–107
empathetic, 107–108
Logic, 1, 21–22, 102
Logos, connection and, 101–104,
106–107, 110–113, 175
Low-tech backup plans, 146–147
Low-tech visual aids, 88–89, 93, 96
Lublin, Nancy, 134–135

Mannerisms, 121
Manuscript format, 9
McMillen, Brad, 13–14
Meanings, 117
body language and, 127–128
intention and, 123
Memorized format, 9–10
Memory
of audience, 61, 70, 86
message and, 75
recall and, 7–8, 61, 150
Mental outlines, 7, 60
Mentors, 79
Message, 48, 75, 101
authenticity of, 103–104
balance in, 35–36
craft of, 1, 19–22, 24, 80, 167–168
credibility and, 34
dress and, 129, 137–138
impact of, 57

204 INDEX

Message (*continued*)
 interest in, 82–83
 nonverbals and, 117–118
 persuasion and, 21, 29
Metaphor, 78
Methodology, of studies, 179–182
Mind, frame of, 4, 12
Mindset, creative, 79–80
The Mirror Has Two Faces, 80–82
Mistakes, ix–x, xiv–xv, 167–168,
  170–171, 176. *See also* specific
  topics
 action steps for, 174–176
 self-identification of, xi, xvii
 studies and, xvii–xviii, 179–182
Money argument, 26
Monroe, Alan H., *Principles and Types
  of Speech Communication*, 21.
  See also Motivated Sequence, of
  Monroe
More, Less as, 63, 92
Motivated Sequence, of Monroe, 21,
  29, 71
 Action Step of, 23, 42–44, 49, 58, 106
 Attention Step of, 22, 58
 Need Step of, 22–24, 26–27, 31, 58
 Satisfaction Step of, 23, 31, 58
 Visualization Step of, 23, 43, 58,
  105–106
Movement, 115, 121
 six-point star method of, 123–124
Musk, Elon, 146
My Fair Lady, 155–156, 165

Need Step, of Motivated Sequence,
  22–24, 26–27, 31, 58
Needs, 33
 of audience, 51
 wants and, 24–26

Nervousness, 14, 125
 challenges and, 151
 credibility and, 173
 preparation and, 119, 128, 172–173
Nonverbals, 118. *See also* Body
  language
 awareness of, 120–122
 distraction and, 117, 119–120, 123,
  125–126, 128
 energy and, 124–128
No-tech backup plans, 146–147

Obama, Barack, 77
Objectives, clarity and, 44
Objectivity, 19, 120
Observations, research, xix, 100,
  118–119, 130, 140, 157–164,
  179–181
Offer, of service, 43–44
Off-putting style, 33, 100, 159
 verbal, 155, 163–164
On-camera, practice, 143, 167–172
Opportunities, xi, xv–xvi
 body language and, 120
 challenges and, 64
 close of sale and, 47–48
 delivery and, xx
 frame of mind and, 12
 preparation and, xxi, 48
 verbal skills and, 156
 videoconference presentations
  and, 141
Outcomes, xii, xvi, 12, 151
 arguments and, 21
Outlines, 11, 88
 as backup plan, 146–147, 153
 conversation and, 57, 64
 forms for, 59–61, 63–64, 66–69,
  71, 175

mental, 7, 60
time allotment and, 54, 57–61,
    63–64, 66–70
written, 7–8
Overconfidence, 3, 108–109, 163
Overnight presentations, 63, 71

Pace, verbal skills and, 158, 161–163
Pain points, xii
    humor and, 93–94
Pandemic. *See* Coronavirus pandemic
Passion, xiii, 38–40, 80, 102
Pasternak, Anna, 162
Pasteur, Louis, 167
Pathos, connection and, 101–103,
    110–113, 175
Pauses, in delivery, 158, 163, 173
Perfection, xii, xxi, 165, 176
Performance, 31, 157, 168–179
    visual aids as, 85
Personality, xx, 27, 110, 115, 164
Personification, 77
Persuasion, ix, xvi, xx, 7, 9
    clarity and, 18–19
    close of sale and, 42, 46
    connection and, 100–101, 148
    information overload compared to,
        xviii, 17–18, 20, 28
    message and, 21, 29
    visual aids and, 86, 88, 90
Pivots, 4, 7
    coronavirus pandemic and, 93–96
    demonstration failures and,
        151–152
    strategy for, 42, 45–46, 49
    visual aids and, 93–94
Polish, ix, xxi
    practice and, 174
    professionalism and, 119–120, 122

Pozner, Barry Z., *Credibility*, 34
Practice, xx, 4, 15, 176
    body language and, 121–122
    clarity and, 161–162
    colleagues and, 9–12, 120, 144,
        168, 172–173
    feedback and, 167–171, 174
    improvement and, 151, 171
    on-camera, 143, 167–172
    polish and, 174
    scrimmage as, 11–12
    time constraints and, 167–168
    videoconference presentations and,
        141–142
Precision, 8–9, 34
Preparation, xi, 4–5, 165
    of answers, 10, 13
    backup plans and, 146
    connection and, 108
    human error and, 150
    improvisation and, 3, 11, 15
    nervousness and, 119, 128,
        172–173
    opportunity and, xxi, 48
    outlines and, 57
    specificity and, 9–10
    spontaneity and, 13
    technology and, 142–145
    time constraints and, 13–14, 54
    visual aids and, 86, 88, 96
    visualization and, 151
Presentation formats, xix, 15, 28, 45,
    54
    demonstration failures and,
        140–141
    dress and, 131–132
Presentation Opportunity General
    Information Form, 5–6, 12,
    63–65, 71, 174

206 INDEX

Presentation Outline Worksheet, 59–60, 175

Presentation Outline Worksheet (Long Version), 60–61, 63, 66–68, 71

Presentations, ix. *See also* Conclusion; Videoconference presentations; Virtual presentations
  body of, 58, 60–61, 86, 124
  boring, xviii, 77–79
  categories of, 19–20
  components of, 56, 58–61, 66–69, 71
  general, 26–27, 64–65, 71
  hybrid, xix, 119–120, 148–149, 153, 180–181
  in-person, xix, 4, 45, 53–55, 75–76, 180–181
  introduction of, 56, 58, 60–61, 124
  overnight, 63, 71
  research in, 36–37
  rushed, 55, 62
  tailored, 10, 28, 56, 159

Presenter, 74
  energy of, 12, 73, 80–82

Principles and Types of Speech Communication (Monroe), 21

Problem-solving, 22, 31

Procrastination, 3
  flow and, 5

Productivity, 26, 110

Profanity, 159–160

Professionalism, 128, 153
  competence and, 129, 141, 155
  dress and, 131–132
  polish and, 119–120, 122
  style and, 163–164

Professionals, sales, x, xvi, xix, 19, 80, 105, 179–181

Progression, of sale, 14, 23, 42, 124
  outlines and, 57

Promotion, close of sale and, 44

Pronunciation, 156, 160–162

Proof
  evidence and, 31–32
  social, 31, 36, 38

Publilius Syrus, xvi

Pygmalion (Shaw), 155–156

Quantified improvement, 31

Qubein, Nido R., 131

Questions
  assumptions and, 106
  audience, 23, 25
  rhetorical, 77

Rapport, 55, 99, 148. *See also* Connection

Read the room, 54, 99, 113, 164

Recall, 7–8, 61, 150

Recording, 171
  of body language, 120, 126
  of verbal skills, 157–158

Redundancy, of words, 157–158

Reflections, xvi, 78, 181–182
  body language and, 119–120, 122–124
  boring presentations and, 74–76, 80–82
  close of sale and, 42–43, 45
  connection and, 102–103, 106–109
  demonstration failures and, 142, 146–147
  dress and, 131–133
  human error and, 148–151
  improvisation and, 4–5, 11–12
  information overload and, 18–21

INDEX **207**

support and, 32–33, 35–36
technology failures and, 142,
146–147
time allotment and, 54–55, 57, 62
verbal skills and, 157–164
visual aids and, 86–88, 90–96
Refresh, of body language, 121–122,
126
Rejection, fear of, 41, 49
Relationship, 43–44, 100, 106–107
data and, 35
Remote audiences
eye contact and, 149
tools and, 148–149
Repetition, 77, 158
Research, 182
observations in, xix, 100, 118–119,
130, 140, 157–164, 179–181
in presentations, 36–37
stories and, 78
Respect
dress and, 133
time and, 55, 62
verbal skills and, 160
Restlessness, 118–120
Return, on investment, 36
Review, 171
of body language, 119, 120–121,
123, 126
Rhetoric (Aristotle), 101–102, 104,
110, 112
Rhetorical devices, 76–78
Rhetorical question, 77
Rhetorical triangle, 101–102, 110
Risk, 41, 132, 151–152
Royal Society Open Science study,
122
Rules, of visual aids, 92, 98
Rushed presentations, 55, 62

Sales. *See also* Close, of sale
ethics in, 33–34
progression of, 14, 23, 42, 57, 124
Sales professionals, x, xvi, xix, 19, 80,
105, 179–181
Samples, 89, 151
San Diego State University, x–xi
Sanity argument, 26
Satisfaction Step, of Motivated
Sequence, 23, 31, 58
Scientific American, 127
Scrimmage, 167
as practice, 11–12
Scripts, 103, 163
Security argument, 26–27
Self-assessment, 158, 171
Self-identification, of mistakes, xi, xvii
Self-talk, 12–13
Selling points. *See* Arguments
Seneca, xi, 48
Sensory experiences, 86, 88
Service, offer of, 43–44
Setting, in virtual presentations, 143
Shaw, George Bernard, *Pygmalion*,
155–156
Short Outline Form, 64, 69
Show, tell and, 38, 98
Shu, Suzanne B., 60–61
Similarities, 76, 78
Simple Video & Tech-Ready
Checklist, 143–145
Simplicity, 21, 93–94, 147
visual aids and, 92
Six-point star method, of movement,
123–124
Skills, xvii. *See also* Verbal skills
analysis of, 168
delivery, 155, 166
Slide shows, 89, 97

208 INDEX

"So what?" test, 24–26, 29, 31, 168
Social proof, 31, 36, 38
Solutions
  arguments and, 26
  balance and, 39
  mistakes and, xiv–xv
  for problems, 22, 31
  Satisfaction Step and, 23
Sound, in videoconference
    presentations, 144
Specificity, 29, 40
  arguments and, 24–26
  of ask, 43–44
  audience and, 38
  brevity and, 28
  logos and, 103
  preparation and, 9–10
Speech formats, 11
  extemporaneous, 8–9
  impromptu, 7–8
  manuscript, 9
  memorized, 9–10
Speech supports, 75–77
  entertainment and, 80
  evidence and, 78, 82
  understanding and, 74, 82
Spontaneity, 9
  preparation and, 13
State of Sales Presentations study,
    x–xi, xvi–xix, 179–182. *See also*
    Reflections
Statistics
  credibility and, 37
  strategy and, 39–40
Stereotypes, 100
Stiff delivery, 9, 119, 126, 164
Stone, W. Clement, 47
Stories, 61, 70
  humor and, 81

research and, 78
Storytelling
  anecdotes and, 76
  boredom and, 73
  creativity and, 51
  data and, 75, 104
  evidence and, 32, 35–36, 39, 40
  pathos and, 102–104
  reflections on, 78
  visualization and, 105–106
Strategy
  balance and, 39
  dress and, 133
  pivot, 42, 45–46, 49
  statistics and, 39–40
  technology and, xv
Stress, 26, 93, 136, 172–173
Structure, 51, 56, 58–61, 66–69, 71
Studies
  mistakes and, xvii–xviii, 179–182
  research observations in, xix, 100,
    118–119, 130, 140, 157–164,
    179–181
  of Royal Society Open Science,
    122
  State of Sales Presentations, x–xi,
    xvi–xix, 179–182
  Wharton School of Business,
    87
Style, 115, 118
  accents and, 156
  clarity and, 164
  of dress, 132, 136
  function and, 129
  informal, 131, 163–164
  off-putting, 33, 100, 155, 159
  verbal, 155–157, 163–164
Suits, 132–136
Summary, of presentations, 61

INDEX 209

Superlatives, 25
Support, 34, 171. *See also* Speech
    supports
  data as, 37
  decisions and, 31
  demonstrations as, 38
  inadequate, 31–33
  passion and, 38–40
  reflections on, 32–33, 35–36
  surveys as, 36–38
  testimonials as, 37–38, 40
  video as, 38
  visual aids and, 86–87, 93
Surveys, x, 179, 181–182
  as support, 36–38

Tailored presentations, 10, 28, 56,
  159
Talk
  close, 119, 126
  to self, 12–13
Talking points, 70
  balance of, 56
  unique, 21–26
Technology, ix, xix
  preparation and, 142–145
  strategy and, xv
Technology failures, 88–89, 96,
  139–141
  focus and, 150–151
  reflections on, 142, 146–147
  Simple Video & Tech-Ready
    Checklist for, 143–145
TED Talks, 104
Tedium, 73, 82
Tell, show and, 38, 98
Templates, 6, 59, 63–69
Test, "so what?," 24–26, 29, 31,
  168

Testimonials
  credibility and, 36–37
  as support, 37–38, 40
Text, in visual aids, 90–92
Therapy, 172
Thomas, Dylan, 80
Thought, 22, 23, 75, 82
Time
  adaptation and, 55
  anecdotes and, 76
  argument of, 26
  balance and, 71, 73
  clarity and, 54–57, 70
  content and, 56–57
  effectiveness and, 54, 62–70
  respect and, 55, 62
  visual aids and, 86, 90, 93
Time allotment, 53, 65, 71
  close of sale and, 62
  outlines and, 54, 57–61, 63–64,
    66–70
  reflections on, 54–55, 57, 62
Time constraints, 8, 11, 55
  audience and, 53–54
  practice and, 167–168
  preparation and, 13–14, 54
Tone, 93, 117, 162–163
  dress and, 134
Tools
  remote audiences and, 148–149
  visual aids as, 88–90, 93, 96
Trade shows, 95–96
Training, xvii, 9, 151
Transitions, 43, 60, 123–124, 163
Trial and error, xiv, 155, 166
Truman, Harry S., 39
Trust, 176
  connection and, 102
  likeability and, 109–110

210 INDEX

Trust (*continued*)
  needs and, 33
Trusted Leader (Horsager), 110

Uncertainty. *See* Certainty
Understanding
  adaptation and, 100
  of audience, 33, 74
  speech supports and, 74, 82
Unique talking points, 21–26
Unprofessional dress, 129–130, 138

Value, 31, 40, 88
Values, 20, 99, 103, 109
Verbal clarity, 157, 160–162
Verbal skills, 165–166
  awareness and, 156–157
  credibility and, 155–156
  customized content and, 158–159
  pace and, 158, 161–163
  reflections on, 157–164
  respect and, 160
Verbal style, 156–157
  off-putting, 155, 163–164
Video, 89
  as support, 38
Videoconference presentations,
    180–181
  backup plans for, 144, 146–147
  close of sale and, 54
  creativity and, 75–76
  dress and, 130–132
  home studios and, 95–96
  practice and, 141–142
  Simple Video & Tech-Ready
    Checklist for, 143–145
  time constraints and, 53–55
  visual aids and, 94–96
Virtual eye contact, 143

Virtual presentations, xi, xix, 11,
    149. *See also* Videoconference
    presentations
  dress and, 131
  in-person and, 4
  setting in, 143
Virtual workplaces, xviii, 180
Visual aids, 51, 89, 97, 143
  audience and, 87, 90–94, 98
  bullet point lists as, 90–94
  clarity and, 88, 92
  connection and, 110
  design of, 92, 111
  engagement and, 86–87, 94–96
  enhancement and, 86, 88, 92, 96
  as performance, 85
  reflections on, 86–88, 90–96
  rules of, 92, 98
  support and, 86–87, 93
  time and, 86, 90, 93
Visual appeal, 87–88
Visual experiences, 38
Visualization
  preparation and, 151
  storytelling and, 105–106
Visualization Step, of Motivated
    Sequence, 23, 43, 58, 105–106
Vocabulary, 158–159
Volume, of delivery, 162–163

Wants, needs and, 24–26
Wharton School of Business, 87
Wickman, Floyd, 63
"Winging it," xv, xviii. *See also*
    Improvisation
  clarity and, 11
  nonverbals and, 125
Words, xiii
  anchor, 60

filler, 155, 157–158, 166
   redundancy of, 157–158
Workplaces, virtual, xviii, 180
Wow factor, 31, 87–89, 92, 139
Written outlines, 7–8

Ziglar, Zig, 63
Zoom, 55, 89, 180. *See also*
   Videoconference presentations

About the Author

Terri L. Sjodin is one of America's leading experts on persuasive presentations. More than thirty years after launching her company, Sjodin Communications, from a spare room in her home, she has built an impressive client list that includes Fortune 500 companies, small businesses, national sales teams, industry associations, and even members of Congress.

Her specialty is blending communications theory, field research, and practical sales experience to help professionals become more polished, persuasive presenters in an ever-changing marketplace. Terri combines a fresh approach and sassy style with highly effective, road-tested solutions for busy salespeople, entrepreneurs, executives, and anyone else who needs to speak well under pressure.

Terri is a *New York Times* bestselling author, an award-winning speaker, a popular LinkedIn Learning Instructor, and a frequent guest on radio and television talk shows throughout the country, appearing on *The Today Show*, Bloomberg, CNN, CNBC, and many industry podcasts.

Online Video Class Option

You can view Terri's LinkedIn Learning course, "Sales Skills: 12 Common Mistakes to Avoid in Your Next Persuasive Presentation," on the LinkedIn Learning platform.

Length: 34 minutes
Level: Beginner

For more information, please visit www.sjodincommunications.com.